Sharing and Caring-

The Key to Taking Your Business Up, Up and Away

By Ilene Meckley

A Meckley Publication

Table of Contents

Dedication...v

Acknowledgments..........................…..……...vii

Chapter 1 My Introduction to Sales..................1

Chapter 2 How Do You Determine What Your
"ALL" Is.........................…...................11

Chapter 3 The Three P's: Purpose, Passion
and Plan........................…......…...........19

Chapter 4 Making a Commitment..................39

Chapter 5 Face Your Fears..........................55

Chapter 6 Why Sales?.................................71

Chapter 7 Prospecting—Opening the Doors to
New Opportunities.....................…...........83

Chapter 8 The Language of Recruiting
(or Ilene's Steps to Success).......................117

Chapter 9 Creating a Work Environment.........149

Chapter 10 My Husband and My Father
Speak Out...157

Chapter 11 Finally, It's Up to You.................167

Appendix A Action Plan............................173

Appendix B Spiral Notebook......................175

Appendix C Success Notes.........................179

Appendix D Suggested Reading List..............182

Dedication

This book is dedicated to some very special people in my life. First, there is my husband, Jim, who knew I could be successful having my own business and who continues to encourage and support me every day of my life. To my five children—Adena, Stephanie, David, Sammy, and Michael—who have been the reasons I worked hard at my business every day for the last 13 years, I am deeply indebted to them for their help and love. For my parents, who always have made me feel that I could be a success, and my grandparents, who had their own business and really role modeled for me that developing relationships with my customers is important in business, I am especially grateful. Gramma, you always said I should go into business!

Acknowledgments

Having a business where I can feel I have been able to have it all would have never happened without the help of many people. First, I am so thankful to Lane Nemeth, founder of Discovery Toys, Inc., who really helped me realize how important it is to dream, set goals and to make things happen. After many happy years with Discovery Toys, Inc., I was approached by a headhunter to work for another company in a corporate position. Lane helped me recognize that I could really be sharing my love of recruiting and helping others while having my own business instead of having to work for someone else. This allows me to pursue two of my passions, developing my own business while teaching others to develop their own businesses too.

Other special people helped me along the way—there was Bonnie Nelson, who believed in me before I believed in myself, and Leslie Ann Williams, who taught me what coaching was all about as opposed to just being a cheerleader. I also want to thank my entire sales team and everyone who has been a part of my business throughout the years. Special thanks go to my first National Sales Director Randi Freed-Cohen and my fabulous first High Five group, Lisa Ashworth, Carol DeSoto,

Cathy MacCloud, Ilene Martire and Dianne Werner-Taylor, who are really learning what *sharing and caring* is all about.

I particularly want to thank **you,** the reader, and let you know that you are helping my dreams come true by allowing me to share my ideas with you through my books, tapes, and my seminars. You are so much a part of  what I love to do—*sharing my passion about helping others make choices to become involved in a fabulous opportunity in network marketing!*

Chapter 1

My Introduction

to

Sales

Chapter 1

My Introduction to Sales

I am so glad that I decided to work and treat my home-based business as just that—a business—right from the beginning. I knew from the start that my goal was to help people learn about the benefits of the products I sell. I also wanted to share with everyone that there is a great opportunity to earn income not only through selling but also by *sharing* with others the idea that they, too, can join our company. You see, it is important for me not to just **take** my customers' money but instead to also **give** them the opportunity to **earn** money because of my desire to share. Personally helping over 650 people join my sales team has continuously kept me excited about my business. *Sharing and caring* about others is why I have been able to help so many people make the decision to give sales a try.

This book will help others, whether they are single, married, or parents, realize the benefits, the fun, the challenges,  and the impact of a home-based business. Even if you are not a parent, you will be meeting lots of parents who will be glad to know you have the insight into a family, home-based business.

In 1985, I was a working mom with a boss, a husband, and five children ages one to eleven. I was not very happy with my working situation and needed to make a change. At the time, I was coordinating a United Way agency's family day care program. One of my responsibilities was to help families find good day care and help ease them into feeling comfortable about leaving their children and going back to work. I knew it was definitely time to make a personal change when the moms I was talking to were crying because they were leaving their babies—and I would cry too! I knew I didn't want a job where I had no choices when it came to spending time with my children. So I took a step many people probably would not have dared to take; I made the decision to change my situation immediately.

I called my husband, Jim, and asked him if there was any way we could afford for me to quit work. He said, "I'm sure we can find a way." That was good enough for me to call my supervisor and say, "I'm out of here!" It felt great! I could hardly wait for that evening to talk with Jim about how great I was feeling. He came home and said, "We need to find time tonight to talk about how we can afford for you to quit work." "OOPS!" I thought, and then said, "We won't need *much* time because I've already quit."

You see I had forgotten that our mortgage company and the department stores where we had charge accounts wouldn't care that I quit work. The monthly payments still had to be made. Jim, being a supportive husband, reassured me that we would find a way to make this work out by meeting our obligations solely from his income.

I became the "Super Mom," constantly reading to the kids, playing with them, baking with them, and really trying to make up for the time together that I felt that we had lost. Looking back now, I think they were probably cheering at  naptime, "Yea, we finally get a break from Mom!" And of course, I wanted to be "Super Wife" too, keeping the house looking great and preparing good meals for Jim when he came home. I was basically spending time doing things, around the house and with the kids, I felt I never previously had the time to do. However, the bills kept coming. I kept hoping the creditors would realize I no longer had a paycheck—and the bills would just disappear. Unfortunately, I couldn't just wish them away.

One day I called Frances, my children's former day care provider, and asked her if the boys and I could come over to play. She said, "You really must be bored and desperate to want to come over here and spend the day with me and all these children." Thinking back to that day, I realize that most of my friends were working, we had no extra money to spend, and I was really searching for something! I enjoyed being a stay-at-home mom but *something* was missing in my life. I also realized that I didn't want my kids to see my role as just the cook and housekeeper. As their chief role model, being the parent at home, I guess I was really searching for a way to have it "ALL." I wanted to be able to do those "mom" things that I chose to do, when I wanted to do them, and find a good housekeeper to do the rest.

Who would have thought that the day I was visiting Frances would become the day I began to find out that I can have it "ALL" and not have **anything** missing? While I was visiting her, she suggested I sell the educational toys that I had previously told her about. I instantly thought, "Why would she say that? What did she think about me? Why did she think I would be good in sales?" Well, I took my kids and went home, feeling rather insulted. Later, I discovered I could be the kind of salesperson **I** would want helping me, and not be the stereotypical salesperson I was thinking about then. Did you have that reaction when someone suggested you go into sales?

That night after dinner, I shared Frances' suggestion with Jim, expecting him to say, "Why would she suggest that to you?" To my surprise, he replied, "What a great idea!" I immediately went through the same negative thoughts I had earlier that day when Frances made the suggestion to me. In addition, I wondered why Jim, after being married to me for twelve years, would think I could be a successful salesperson. In fact, he knew I was rather shy.

Well, they were both right. I *was* cut out for sales, although it took me a while to discover my real potential that led to the techniques I will share with you in this book.

You might be asking, "Why is this mother of five writing a book, making tapes and doing seminars?" I can tell you why *so* easily. I have always felt that when you find out about something good, it is your obligation to share it with others and not just keep it to yourself. Why would anyone ever want to keep anything so good a secret? I have found something great that I want to share, and I wanted to find a

7

way to share it with more people than I could ever meet personally. You see I'm a mom and wife who really feels like I can have it "ALL." "ALL" is something very personal, something we each define for ourselves. The bottom line is that when we have it "ALL," we feel very good about ourselves and are very happy with our lives.

As I have mentioned before, my "ALL" had to include being the best wife and mom that I could be. I realized as a mom that I should also be a role model that would help my children develop into confident and successful adults who themselves will one day be great parents of my future grandchildren. Fortunately, I was able to reach that goal, and my children have grown up seeing their mom become a successful businessperson! The role modeling became my principal driving force to be successful.

My hope is that **you will** define what **your "ALL"** is—and that with my encouragement through this book, you will have the determination and desire to try the new things that I will be suggesting so that you too will be able to achieve your "ALL." Then you also will really feel you have something important to share with others through your home-based business. Remember that my creed, **"Recruiting Starts With *Sharing And***

8

Caring," is an important key to your business success and your ultimate happiness. My ultimate happiness has been to watch and be a significant part of my wonderful children's lives. All of my children have learned the importance of *sharing and caring*. Adena has dedicated her life to helping others through her career in psychology. Stephanie has just received her degree in social work and has such a gentle manner and love of people. David is a caring college son who is so sensitive to other people's needs. Sam, who is graduating from high school, has so many talents that he loves to share with others, and Michael's teachers and friends have often mentioned to us his sweetness and kindness. I truly believe that my being able to be at home has very positively influenced my children's lives.

Chapter 2

How Do You Determine What Your "ALL" Is?

Chapter 2

How Do You Determine
What Your "ALL" Is?

One of the first things I realized is that the "ALL" you want today may not be the "ALL" you want tomorrow. Each of us individually has different needs, desires, and goals, and at different times in our lives, those needs, desires, and goals vary. In the beginning, my goal in my home-based business was for me to be able to be home with my children and work **alongside** them while also being able to help pay a few bills including our van payment.

As I mentioned earlier, I quit work suddenly—which meant Jim and I had to make some life-style changes. We had to move from our large house to a much smaller house. We also thought we would have to give up traveling, which we loved to do. The dinners out and the family outings were all going to have to happen less often. College education for our children was something we thought was **way** off in the future. I thought we had

it "ALL" at *that time* and the other things could wait.

Fortunately, as I built my business, we realized we could add to the "ALL" we had. That large house we had given up when I quit work really was not what we wanted when compared to the home we have now created. You see, a few years ago we added a 1000 square foot addition to our current home. The space we added made me feel we had it "ALL" again—and much more—compared to the house we gave up.

Let me see if I can paint a picture for you. Jim and I chose to have a large family. We love having our extended family and friends  come to our home to share meals and lots of fun. We now have a room that is the perfect place for us to have our large family get-togethers. In that room we can all be together talking and enjoying each other's company while some of the group are challenging others to a game of pool or playing ping pong, while still others are having fun with "Foosball." In addition, we wanted a place where the kids would always be able to entertain their friends too. For example, we've had a cast party of 50 high school kids and a youth group sleep-over, just to name a couple of happenings. Dinner in our home often involves twenty or more people. I almost forgot to mention the two dogs and two cats that are equal members of the family.

Oh yes, there's also our master bedroom that we added with the hot tub right in our room—that's right, not in the bathroom. You see when we were building our addition, I wanted a place for Jim and me to be able to relax and unwind. I did not want to think about the bathroom that needed to be cleaned. I wanted *romance*.

I want to share with you a little story to illustrate how important painting pictures can be.

We told our builder we wanted a large hot tub. He said, "We'll need to make your bathroom larger." I said, "Oh no, we don't want it in our bathroom. We want it in our bedroom!" His answer, spoken with a sheepish grin on his face was, "Oh, I get it. What if I also make a small window above the hot tub so you can look out at the stars?" I replied, "Now you've got it."

I'm sharing some of this with you because I want **you** to realize that you never have to settle for less and you too can have whatever it is that you think is your "ALL."

You know the travel that Jim and I thought we would have to give up? Boy, were we wrong! Since I started my own business, we've been to Hawaii three times, Scotland, the Bahamas, London, Mexico three times, on a cruise, two Club Meds, Canada, Del Coronado, Palm Springs, and many more places. We have traveled to luxurious places we would never have dreamed of going. And, oh yes, the family has seen more places than they would ever have seen if I had not decided to work hard and set goals in my business. Now, I travel all over the country doing seminars, often taking one or more of our grown-up children with me.

As far as the colleges, it is because of my business that Jim and I know that we are able to help with all of our children's college plans.

Do you see how the "ALL" has continued to change? Now, we have a new "ALL." We are working towards Jim's early retirement from his current job so that we can work alongside each

16

other in our home-based business. I want Jim to have the opportunity to see how great it is to be his own boss. At least he'll think he is! (Just joking, Jim.)

I want you to feel confident that you too can reach the heights that you set for yourself. Nothing stands in your way but the "will" and the effort to realize every dream that you have.

Now is the time for you to identify what you want your "ALL" to be—right now—keeping in mind that it **can** and **will** change. The Three Ps, **Purpose, Passion,** and **Plan,** are what have kept me committed to working in my business each day **alongside** my family. Decide right now that you have the ability to reach your goals and make your dreams come true. That is the most important step in deciding what your hopes and dreams really are. **Know it, believe it, and feel it!**

Now you have to be realistic and honestly answer one very important question: Are **you** willing to do what it takes to make it happen? If the answer is yes, then there really is a will and a way. Saying things such as "I hope I reach a goal" or "I'll try" really are not statements of commitment. These statements, that are nothing more than "wishful thinking," indicate that the goal you have

17

set is really not very important to you. Once you set a goal that has *value* and *meaning* to you, then you will find a way to work towards it keeping everything else in your life in balance. When your statement is "I'll do" rather than "I'll try," or "I will" rather than "I hope," then you will have taken the first step to making a commitment to succeed.

Here's an example: when I decided to do training seminars, make training tapes and write a book, I made up my mind to do the very best that I can. I was determined to give it my all. Feeling that way gave me the confidence I needed to get started, and you too can have that same feeling of confidence that you can succeed. If I didn't have the "I can do" feeling, I would still be thinking about: "Can I? Will it work? Or, what if I can't?" I made the decision that **"I can and I will."** Trust me, I believe that anyone reading this book has demonstrated the desire to succeed. Now it's time to work on **your** Three Ps individually, so that you too can express your very personal commitment to yourself that you will succeed.

Chapter 3

The Three P's:

 Purpose,

Passion,

and

 Plan

Chapter 3

The Three Ps:
Purpose, Passion and Plan

Purpose

 What is **your** purpose for your business? What would you like to see it do for you and your family? Is there anything that you would like to have or do now or that you would like to have or do in the future? Where would you like to travel?

How much money do you want to earn weekly, monthly, yearly? In what other career can you decide you want or need more money tomorrow and actually do something about it because the  business is yours? Can you imagine walking into a boss' office and saying, "I really would like to have some money to take my family on a vacation. Can I start making more money tomorrow, please?" In a business like ours—that is *our* business—you can do that. You can make more money tomorrow or even today. Just schedule some more presentations or make a few more contacts, and you're on your way to increasing your income. Have you ever considered how lucky we are that we can decide how much of our time to invest in our businesses based solely on the amount of income we need and desire?

How do you plan to spend the money you earn? Can you see how your income will specifically benefit you and your family? Does each of your family members see the benefits of your work? Can you imagine having your own business bank account from which you pay yourself a salary? As that account grows, your family can see that you really are in business, a business that makes money.

What impact do you see your business having on your family? How do you share your goal setting and business strategies with your family? Do you discuss your business with your "significant other" and your children? Can you see how beneficial it will be for your family to be a part of the planning process? Wouldn't you like your children to grow up knowing how to set goals, a technique they will have learned from observing you and participating with you in your business? They too will learn that they can be successful in reaching their dreams, provided they are willing to plan and work as hard as you are. Isn't this another good reason for you to set goals and design a strategy for success? Your children are watching you!

****

Passion

 It is much easier to enjoy your work when you are excited about what you do. I personally have found a business where I am able to say I love what I do! I may not always love every part of my work; yet, without a doubt, I love sharing information about my company's products and business opportunity. I hope you have the same passion for your company's products and business opportunity! I love talking to others—and by "others" I mean <u>everyone</u>—about joining me on my sales team. Now, through my seminars, I train people who work in many different companies throughout the United States how they too can achieve the same satisfaction from their businesses.

I have learned that all of us in a home-based, network marketing business share some similar passions and purposes, just like all teachers share a love for helping children learn. Some teachers like to work with pre-school children, some with elementary children, some with high school students, and some with college students. We may sell different products, but how we build our businesses and the strategies we can use are very similar.

I am very passionate about the products I sell and feel so confident about the products I represent. How do you let potential customers and recruits know that you feel the same way about your products? I want to be sure others know how the products I sell can benefit them, their family, and their friends. What do you do to share the benefits of purchasing your products or joining your company? Sharing with others the benefits of the products and the company in which you believe is one of the most valuable keys to success. This leads to their making the decision to invest in your products and to join you in your business opportunity.

In a business where we are not only sharing a product but a business opportunity as well, it is extremely important that you make sure you are demonstrating the **real benefits** of your business that your potential representatives can enjoy too. That is where your passion for your business and not just your products comes in to play. My own passion for my business is what  drives me to share the business opportunity to work with the company that I represent. With every passing day and with every contact I make; my passion for the business grows.

My goal now is to give that passion to as many people as I can in network marketing. Wouldn't it be great for our potential customers to think of us *first,* as a source for their shopping needs, before they make that trip to the Mall? After all, buying from us means no hassle in the parking lot, and *lots* of customer service. This is particularly important in today's society where so many people work longer hours than ever before, leaving them no time to take those shopping trips.

Now let's get to the place where you have to be true to yourself and see whether or not you have the passion necessary to make it in your own business. (This means that if you are not as passionate about your business as you are about chocolate you don't have to read any further.)

Take some time to answer the questions below. Some may not be easy for you to answer, and you may have to spend some time thinking about them because they can make such a *big* difference in your sales results as well as in your recruiting results. The passion **you** personally bring to your business determines the energy and enthusiasm with which you approach your business each day. Grab a piece of paper and answer some of the Passion questions!

Why did you choose the particular product line and company you represent as a vehicle to achieve your goals (purpose)?

What about your business excites you every day?

What do you hope to make better for others through your business?

How do you share your passion with family, friends, and others? How do you communicate the fact that you love your work?

Why would people want to join your sales team—what benefits do they gain from working with you and your company?

How would someone complete this sentence about you? "(Your name) really loves her/his business because she/he loves...." Do people say to you, "You must really love your work?" If they don't say you really love your work, why not? If you cannot answer this one with an enthusiastic yes, does this mean you are more passionate about chocolates than your business?

Every business has a bottom line—a measure of success. How are you going to evaluate your business to be sure it is growing and changing to meet **your** bottom line? You need to plan, plan, plan!

****

27

Plan

Did someone tell you that you don't have a boss in a home-based business? In a home-based  business there is still a boss. Guess who it is? **YOU!** Are you going to be an understanding boss, but not one who just says that you don't have to work today without a very good reason? I sure hope so. Are you going to be a boss with expectations? Don't overlook this one—now go back and read the previous question again, for without expectations you can never have a successful business. You do not grow and build a business without expectations and, naturally, a business plan. Are you going to be a boss that requires you to go to work? You do *not* usually get paid for *not* working. (*Not, not*? Who's there? *Not* the money!) Most importantly, are you a boss that is proud of the work that is being done by your favorite employee—YOU?

Now is the time for the good news. We can always be sure the work we are doing is something of which we can be proud since "we" are our own boss and do not have to depend on other people. You may be thinking, "Well, we do depend on other people—the members of our team." That is right, but if we don't like the way our team is performing, it is up to us to recruit new people and role model the individual performance that we would like to see in each of our team members. We are the ones doing the work and also the ones who can change what we are doing at any time.

The key to being your own successful boss is a WORK PLAN and being flexible with that plan; just not too flexible so that you end up "flexing" yourself right out of business. Now we're talking about real Work Plans—just like those found in General Motors, only slightly scaled down—but they are still Work Plans to be taken seriously and followed. There is a real difference between deciding *when* to work on your business and *whether* to work on your business at all. If you find yourself making choices as to whether or not to work at all, it sounds like you have a hobby. Remember that hobbies cause you to <u>spend</u> money. A business is designed to <u>make</u> you money.

Take a look at your daily plan to build your business. Remember that you are your own boss who can determine your own paycheck. If things are not going well, you know to whom to talk—the

29

boss! (Go easy now because the boss is you.) If you find yourself talking to yourself *frequently* about the problems in your business, it's time for you to get serious and take a good hard look at what you are doing.

Seriously consider the following questions. How many people do you want to reach every day? Have you planned to make enough contacts to get you where you want to go in your business? Are you taking advantage of your daily routine to include prospecting—*sharing and caring* enough to take time to share information about your company's products and business opportunity with the people you contact?

Are you prepared with business cards and other important information to share with others? What do you share about your business when you meet someone new? Do you always include in the conversation "One of the things I love to do is help others start their own home-based businesses too"?

 How do you keep track of the customers coming through your business every day? Do you keep a log to be able to really evaluate your daily contacts? Are you happy with what you see in your log?

Do you have a follow-up system for new prospects and leads?

How many sales events and recruiting appointments do you want to have each day, each week?

****

Let's talk about the Three Ps when working at home with your children.

When you have children at home, you have to make plans to work **alongside** the children. Babies can sit in your arms or in an infant seat while you make one or two calls every hour (total of ten minutes on the phone at the most), watch you smile, and feel your touch—they will think you are talking to them. Trust me, my oldest daughter Adena, who just received her Master's degree and is now working on her Doctorate in psychology, heard my voice reading notes from a psychology class I was taking when she was three months old. Think it has anything to do with her interests? Possibly not, but my point is that she was happy and I was able to do the work I was required to do. It worked out for both of us.

Preschoolers need to learn that they can't always have our attention. That's a fact of life in getting along in our society. Can you imagine what happens in school when a child who is accustomed to his mother's undivided attention finds out the teacher has to share class time with 30 other students? Wouldn't you like your children to be prepared to enter the community of pre-school kids without suffering from "traumatic missing Mom syndrome?" This syndrome starts with being a "smother mother," a mother who feels she has to be her child's constant companion and entertainer. This will make it difficult for a child to develop any independence and self-assurance.

I often hear parents say that the minute they get on the telephone their kids begin to "act out" and get into trouble. This translates into lots of noise while Mom is on the telephone making that important business call. What would happen if you decided to make your **phone time** a **fun time** for your children? What if you told your children every time you were about to get on the phone that they are going to get to do something special? That means you have to do some planning. Sometimes it means you bring out a special toy that is not available to them all the time, making it like a new toy each time. Maybe the next time you will have an art project ready for them to do while you are on the phone or as soon as you hang up.

Just try this with *your* young children. Tell them you have something special they get to do while you are on the phone and then, after you hang up, be sure to reinforce their good behavior with lots of praise. Then do something *with them* for a few minutes. They will begin to learn the ritual and see how great phone time can be. Really, this is not only important to your business but it's generally good behavior for children not to be screaming while their parents are on the telephone. It does take planning and follow-through on your part. Make **Phone Time is Fun Time** a motto at your house.

Explain to older children that you in fact work, just like someone who goes to an office outside the home. Be sure they understand the benefits of your work and the rewards the family receives as a result of your being able to be on the phone. Just think, three calls every hour keeping them to five minutes each is only fifteen minutes an hour. Do that five times a day and you are up to fifteen contacts a day in addition to all those people you encounter throughout your daily routine.

As far as teens are concerned, they should easily comprehend the benefits of more money in the family since teens seem to translate all the family's money into cars, clothes, and movies for themselves. My own teenagers, Sam and Mike, and their sister, Stephanie, realizing the benefits of my business, decided on their own to create a work-related coloring/story book called *Just Like Mom* that I now take with me to all of my seminars. The coloring/story book, which teaches kids about the importance of Mom's work and goal setting, has turned out to be a "best seller." It demonstrates to children how to support and be a part of Mom's business. My children dedicated the book to "...all the mothers who work very hard juggling their business and their families."

From *Just Like Mom*

When Mommy makes important calls, I am as quiet as can be.

Try putting five of your business cards in your pocket or purse every time you go out with your children. Frankly, I keep ten or more in mine. Put the cards where your money is and that will remind you to hand one out every time you pay someone.

When you go to the grocery store and reach in your wallet for the money to pay, take out one of your cards and trade it for the change you get back—don't forget, even the checker at the grocery store is a potential recruit. Here is what you might say,

> *Thanks for your help today. I have my own business and I always like to share what I do with others. Have you ever heard of (**your company**)? I would love for you to share some information about my business with others. Have you ever thought about doing something **alongside** what you do now to supplement your income?*

If the lines at the checkouts are long, just hand the card to the cashier with a five-second invitation to call you for more information concerning how she/he can supplement her/his income or order your products. (I have sold products and met potential representatives at the bagel store, in parking lots—yes I share in parking lots too—and at the Post Office.) The more cards you hand out the better.

And don't forget, you can recruit and sell while travelling—one of my best contacts was made at 30,000 feet in the air with a person seated next to me while I was on my way to a recruiting seminar I was presenting. Handing out your business cards works!

 So, what is your plan to work on your business today?

Chapter 4

Making a Commitment

Chapter 4

Making a Commitment

It is important to realize that your Purpose, Passion, and Plan will mean absolutely nothing without total commitment. To me there is a real difference between what I call the "Wannabes" attitude and the "totally committed to do whatever it takes" attitude. I have always wanted to exercise and lower my cholesterol in order to be healthier. Was wanting it good enough? Absolutely not! My own "Wannabe" attitude didn't help me get on the treadmill or avoid unhealthy food. Very recently, I decided I had better apply the principles I follow in my business to my own health. Now, I make time to exercise. I eat a low-fat diet. I make the choices I know will lead me to the results I want to have. Unfortunately, wishing, hoping, and wanting do not cause anything to happen. Doing what *is* necessary does!

How do you determine the strength of your commitment? Are you willing to do those things that will make you a successful businessperson when you don't feel like doing them? (Getting up and exercising at 5:30 a.m. is commitment.) What are you committed to doing to help your business?

Do you say, "I'll try to see if this will work," or do you say, "I am going to find a way to make it work"?

Do you say, "When it happens, it will happen," or do you say, "I will make it happen"?

Do you say, "I'll start tomorrow," or do you say, "I can't wait to get started right away"?

It is very important to be sure that you are honest with yourself about your business. I hear people say all the time, "I can't." When I hear that, an alarm goes off in my head, and I wonder how seriously they take their business. When you find yourself saying that: STOP—THINK! Remember that you **can** do it, and say to yourself, "I **will** do it." Just think, if you have children, would you accept an "I can't" from them?

Do you really treat your business like a business? Do you avoid doing things you would have to do if you were employed in another occupation—you know the kinds of things nobody wants to do? Would you ignore them or go to your boss and say, "I don't like these things—they bore me so I won't do them. Okay?"

Obviously, you wouldn't think of doing that—you would do what you had to do to complete the job and perhaps, more importantly, be able to look in the mirror and say, "I'm doing the best job I can." And, that's exactly the attitude I want to see you have in your own business because I know with that attitude you can be a success.

Don't let fears keep you from doing the things you have to do in your business either. For example, a new nurse would not tell the doctor for whom she is working, "Sorry, I don't feel comfortable giving people shots. I only know how to do oranges." A teacher would not tell the principal, "Sorry, I don't mind talking to the children, but I can't do a back-to-school night presentation to parents." It is important that you overcome any fears that you encounter as you grow your business. It isn't any different than any other job that you wish to be successful doing just because you do it from your home.

Excuse or Truth

Let's talk a little bit more about that negative phrase "I can't." I want to share an acronym I heard. "**I CAN'T**" stands for "**I Certainly Am Not Trying.**" It is important for you to think about how many times you find yourself saying, "I can't." If your child said to you "I can't do my homework," would you just say that it is okay? I don't think so! If your child's assignment is to write each spelling word ten times, would you accept her saying that she is tired and only wants to write them seven times? Think about your business contacts; when you say your plan is to make ten today, do you permit yourself to stop at seven? If so, what behavior are you role modeling for your child?

Take a look at some of the statements below that I have actually heard more times than you can imagine. If you have made one of these statements, ask yourself if there isn't a better way to approach your business and overcome some of the challenges you face.

Do you find yourself saying-

I can't work during the day because of the kids.

Do you know that many people actually choose a home-based business so they **can** be working **alongside** their children? I work hard at my business because of my children. I want to hear parents say that they work their home-based business **because of** their children, not that they **can't** because of them. Do you think it is good for your child to hear that you can't work because of them?

> *I can't work at building my business because I have a full-time job.*

Think about the people in your life who work full-time, who are taking courses at night, or who go straight to a part-time job after working all day. They have made a choice to add something important to their lives. Unfortunately, a choice like that does not offer much flexibility. What if you treated your home-based business in the same way, making a commitment to spend a certain amount of time, while allowing yourself some flexibility?

> *I can't work today because I have a birthday party* (or any other event) *to plan this month.*

Let's get serious about this one. I've planned and held about 75 parties and hosted many, many other celebrations—holidays and such—for family and friends. I have often tried to figure out what it is I must have forgotten to do for all these events—they seemed to come off without a hitch! I never felt that planning—and enjoying—these special times kept me from working my business. Can you imagine walking up to a boss and requesting several weeks off "because I'm having a party"? It really only takes planning and dividing up the tasks to insure a successful event. It is definitely *not* an excuse *not* to work.

I can't work today because I have a new pet.

Would you believe an innocent guinea pig was once used as an excuse? Don't forget these quotes are real. Who could *make up* taking off  work and staying home until your guinea pig feels comfortable enough living with you so that you can go back to work? Do you think that the person who says this is really interested in building a business? On the other hand, does this excuse send out the same message as "I've got to wash my hair"? If you find yourself coming up with these silly excuses, then ask yourself if you are clear about your Purpose, Passion, and Plan for your business. Is what you're doing a spare-time hobby or is it really a business? (If you're going into the guinea pig business, ignore this paragraph.)

I can't work today because I have a cold.

It's important to ask yourself if you are feeling so bad that you would take a day off work if you had a job outside the home, a job where you were accountable to someone else. If the answer is yes, then maybe today is a day to pamper yourself and take a "sick" day off from your own business. If the answer is no, then it's important to be committed to working on your business, even though being at home it would be easier to sit back and do nothing.

An advantage of working from home when you're not feeling well is that you can work a little, rest a little; work a little, rest a little. Being your own boss can be helpful when you can't work up to full capacity.

I can't work today—my child is teething (tired, sick, grumpy, and so forth).

Let's look at still another advantage of working from home. Just imagine if you had to get your child ready for school or day care and then rush off to a job, knowing you had no choice (or at best a difficult choice) and could not stay home. How would you feel? Picture this—your little one has a 101-degree temperature, is crying, and only wants Mommy. Your flexible schedule allows you to do the "doctoring," cuddling, and those other things that will make your child happy.

Here's where the real discipline comes in! You can make your phone calls, prepare your mailings, or do what's necessary while he or she is sleeping. Take advantage of the fact that there are pockets of time during the day when you can make one or two contacts—or with luck, even more! Also, share with your "support system"—spouse, mother, friend, and others—that you could really benefit from having someone help out with the nursing duties for even just one hour in order to free you up to make some contacts. People often want to help and are just waiting to be asked. Don't be bashful. By asking for their help, you may be making them very happy to be of assistance to you.

I can't find the time.

It's time to ask yourself if you really believe your business has importance in your life. Are you clear on your Purpose and Passion? Do you just need to sit down and work on your Plan? Are there pockets of time available that you could put to use?

Are you just waiting for a convenient time? Would spending more time on your business increase your income enough so that you could hire someone to do some of those household chores you dislike? The most important question for you to ask yourself is "Are you determined to find the time that's necessary to be successful?"

I can't earn my company's incentive trip.

Do you feel you deserve to earn this trip? Does the "I can't" mean that you are not willing to do the work required? You know that you can earn your company's trip. Look how many others do— why not you? There are always lots of people in everyone's organization who want to help others succeed and that means you. You might need to improve some of your skills, work harder, and ask for help. But, the help is out there for the asking. Remember—if there truly is a "will," there really is a "way."

****

Here are some more things to think about when measuring your commitment level.

♦ Do you look at the glass as half empty or half full?

♦ Do you want to believe everything can be positive?

♦ Do you tend to always find what's wrong in any situation? Or, are you always looking for what's right?

♦ Do you focus on your weaknesses rather than your strengths? Remember weaknesses accomplish nothing—we live off our strengths.

In order for you to succeed in sales, you need to become the most positive, optimistic and confident person possible. You **must** believe in yourself, your company, and your products. In every business, you should expect disappointments just as there are in everything else in life. How you choose to look at the disappointments will ultimately impact your attitude towards your business life. (Doesn't that apply to life in general?) You can't be successful at anything in life, whether it's work or play, without the basic belief in what you are doing and that *you* can be the one to do it.

For example, if your presentation cancels, you may express your disappointment with, "Oh great, I'm never going to be successful." A better response would be to turn the negative into a positive—that is the lifeblood of a successful businessperson. A better way to look at the cancellation is to think, "I'm sure glad that person, who canceled, didn't waste my time if she was not truly interested." After all, if she is really interested, you will be able to reschedule your presentation with her later. You can still use this time that has become available to find other people who are interested in your products or your company. In fact, this single cancellation could lead to dozens of new leads and appointments, and that is a very positive result.

Treat all of your business disappointments the same way you would any other disappointments in life. When you drop the birthday cake at the party, you don't cancel the party—you simply find an alternative that keeps the party on the move. No tears allowed—only smiles.

When disappointments occur in your business, it is time to pick up the phone and start dialing. Don't "reach for the chocolates"—this really **will** work. Decide no matter what the disappointment is you will always find a way to turn a negative into a positive. In fact, this is my approach to my entire life. Just like in a game, whether you are winning or losing, you still can enjoy playing the game. Being determined that you will enjoy your business as much as you enjoy a game will help you turn any "losses" into "wins." You will certainly feel a lot better.

Don't forget, Babe Ruth, the first home run king who hit 714 home runs in his career, also struck out 1,330 times. That's a lot of disappointments, but they didn't stop him from going up to bat the next time. The point is that the number of times you strike out is meaningless. What counts is the number of times you hit a home run—a home run scores.

After hearing a motivational speaker talk about making every day the best day, I decided to share that concept with my family. Now, when I drop my sons off at school, I ask them what will happen today that will make this their best day. After a couple of days of my doing this, they began to ask me the same question.

One day, when my husband drove them to school, he asked, just as I always do, "What will happen today to make this day your best day?"

When Jim got home that night, he said, "Hey, you forgot to tell me the rules of the 'best day' game. You didn't tell me the kids would ask **me** what was going to happen today to make this **my** best day." Just think, I'm raising my sons to be great husbands who will always be thinking about what will make their wives' day a great day. Try the "best day" game in your family and watch everyone begin to look at each day positively as their best day.

Taking Your Business Up, Up, and Away

Chapter 5

Face Your Fears

Chapter 5

Face Your Fears

Any time I feel a fear coming on, I have conditioned myself to remember another acronym I have heard. **FEAR** stands for **F**alse **E**vidence **A**ppearing **R**eal. I have come to the realization that many fears I had were just that. As President Franklin Delano Roosevelt said, " The only thing we have to fear is fear itself." Think about the number of times that you were afraid something would go wrong and it happened. Often what you fear happens because you are focused on the negative—a self-fulfilling prophecy. If we always take that negative energy and apply it to positive thought, just think how much happier we will be.

My fear of speaking almost kept me from having my "ALL." I am so grateful for what Bonnie Nelson did for me many years ago. I received a call from Bonnie who asked me to speak at a "family meeting" at our company's national convention. I said, "Thanks, but no thanks." Bonnie, using her marketing skills, said that she would come do a training for my team in Maryland if I would speak at her "family meeting." I told her I would have to think about it—the pressure of public speaking was still terrifying for me. Jim, knowing my fear, said he thought it would be a great experience for me and once again encouraged me to do something I was afraid to do. So I decided to say yes; after all, how big could a "family meeting" be?

I went to the convention in California dreading the day I was to speak. Before I was supposed to speak, I went back to my hotel room to be with my daughters and hear them say, "You can do it, Mom." I needed their encouragement. They were so excited when I entered the room. Jim and  the boys had sent flowers to me with a card attached that said, "The boys and I know you can do it." I started to cry and wondered, "How *am* I going to do it?" Armed with the card in my pocket, I got myself together and headed to the room where I was supposed to speak.

I opened the door of the meeting room, looked in, and saw several hundred people. The room looked to me like the Rose Bowl filled to capacity. Being an amateur then at positive self-talk and confidence, I immediately turned and left the room hysterically. Someone followed me out, and seeing my emotional state, she asked me if I had just received bad news. I said, "No, I'm just quitting this company—people make you do things you don't want to do." She asked me to stay right there, immediately ran back into the room, and got Bonnie, who came running after me.

Bonnie asked me if instead of speaking to the group, I would just answer questions. She made it clear I would not have to give a talk. I said," No!" She then asked if I would just come into the room, stand up and introduce myself—say, "My name is Ilene Meckley, and I'm from Bowie, Maryland." I said, "No." Finally, she asked, "Would you please just come in the room and stand up when *I* call your name—you just have to stand; that's all." After a few seconds' thought, wanting to deserve my flowers and still clutching the card in my pocket, I finally said, "Yes."

When we went into the room, I was terrified. I was nervously waiting for my name to be called when suddenly I heard ILENE MECKLEY, BOWIE, MARYLAND. I stood up and sat down *so fast* I doubt the people next to me even knew that I had moved. That was my first growth step, or my first growth "stand" I should say.

After the meeting, I tried to leave the room as fast as I could go when I heard my name called again. "Oh, no," I thought. "It's Bonnie." She approached me and said that she was surprised that I wouldn't share with the others how I had been so successful in the first year of my business. She said, "After talking to you this past year, I never thought of you as being selfish." Ouch, that hurt. I never thought of myself as being selfish either, and I said to Bonnie that I am not selfish.

Bonnie replied that she hoped I would learn not to worry about what people were thinking about me; that it was much more important to think about what I could share with them. Being the good coach that she was, she said she would give me another opportunity to share my experience with another group. Wanting to be supportive, she offered to fly across the country, to be there when I spoke, to stand behind the podium, and to hold my hand if necessary. Boy, did that put me on the spot! How could I say no? She would have been right—it would have been selfish of me not to share.

Bonnie did come to help me with my presentation just as she had promised, and I managed to get through it. I also learned an important lesson that some of us refer to as **F. A. Y. C.:** **F**orget **A**bout **Y**ourself **C**ompletely. We should focus on the needs of others instead of worrying about what they might be thinking about us.

Shortly thereafter, I was asked to speak again in Philadelphia. I stood behind the podium with my notes laid out in front of me. Still suffering from some fear, but eager to do particularly well since I had invited my brother to hear my presentation, I grasped the podium and began to speak. Someone noticed the podium was in the wrong position. Another helpful person came up to move the podium thinking I would pick up the microphone in my hand, making the move an easy one. Instead, my hands were locked onto the podium; I was not about to let go. As a result, the podium fell and my notes were scattered all over the floor. There I was—no podium, no notes, and an audience waiting for me to speak. I could see panic on many of their faces—many of them knew of my fear of public speaking. Deciding to ignore my scrambled notes on the floor, I just began to talk and out came those thoughts that I really knew so well—no notes, just sharing what I knew and felt.

As I was talking and sharing, I slowly began to forget about my fears. I had experienced personal growth and had expanded my comfort zone. Bonnie was right about F. A. Y. C. I focused on the task at hand rather than myself and it worked. That was my freedom day from the terrified feelings I had about public speaking.

If public speaking was a problem for me, flying to those speeches was even worse. The idea of having 30,000 feet of airspace between the ground and me was not terribly comforting. That fear almost kept me from a lot of great experiences, including meeting lots of nice people while I was leading seminars all over the country. What fabulous vacations my family and I would have missed if I had not gotten over that fear.

Once, when flying to Canada and really feeling very uncomfortable about the flight, I was concerned about how I was going to get myself back on the plane. I called my husband and he recommended that I get a good book, one that would be encouraging and motivational. I went to the airport bookstore and purchased *Feel the Fear and Do It Anyway* by Susan Jeffers. As we taxied down the runway, my white-knuckled fingers tightly held the book that was supposed to quiet my fears and make this a peaceful flight.

Fear must have been written all over my face because the man sitting next to me said, "Does that book have anything to do with your fear of flying?" Had he been looking at my knuckles, he would have had no doubt at all. After I replied, "Yes," he said, "You'd better be a speed reader because the plane is about to take off." Reading

Jeffers' book enabled me to start controlling my fears. Believing in my ability to handle my fears coupled with Jeffers' message, I made it home safely and most importantly, comfortably.

For some years after that incident, I continued to fly with a lot less fear but still, flying never became  my favorite form of transportation. One day while on a very turbulent flight, a man sitting next to me asked me if I was nervous. It must have been those white knuckles again. When I responded "Yes," he said, "I'm a pilot and I have to tell you that pilots don't get nervous when we experience turbulence. It's really okay. My advice to you is to just feel the bumps and let them rock you to sleep." His advice must have worked because I do not experience the terrible fear I used to have. But, I do seem to spend a lot more time sleeping on planes now.

One of my purposes in writing this book is to be *your* "pilot" on *your* "flight" to a successful business by sharing with you how to overcome the "turbulence" that may come your way. We all know that we are going to experience minor bumps on any journey but we can still arrive safely.

When you have a concern, you have to

determine whether the concern is because of a fear of yours or a lack of desire. Fears can be met head-on and conquered because you have the desire to succeed. Lack of desire raises a different problem—whether or not you really want to be successful and do what it takes to succeed. If the latter is the case, get off the plane as soon as possible. Don't waste any more of your time and the time of others on the trip. For those who are continuing on the journey, let's think about some of the "fears" you or others may encounter in building your business.

➢ What keeps you from talking about your business to the person next to you while you are both waiting in the grocery line?

➢ Why didn't you tell the person sitting next to you at the PTA meeting how much you love your business and how much you would like her to join you?

➢ Why didn't you ask the receptionist in your doctor's office if you could leave promotional materials in the office? Did you think about asking the receptionist to join your business?

➤ Why are you afraid to make that telephone call that you know might lead to a recruit or a sale?

➤ Have you told all your neighbors that they too can make money doing what you do and that you can supply a product to them that they need?

➤ Have you been afraid to ask your best friend from school to join you because you are afraid she'll say no? Have you asked the members of your family if they would be interested in selling and recruiting?

Now here is an *important* one.

➤ Have you been hesitant to ask your "significant other" and members of your family for their assistance in making your business flourish?

These are just some questions that we all need to consider. I hope they will aid you in overcoming some of your fears or concerns. You might want to grab a piece of paper now and list out your specific fears so that you can confront them as I have done.

We've been talking about *your* fears, the fears of people already in the business. Now let's raise some of the thoughts, concerns and questions that go through the minds of people who are thinking about starting a network marketing business.

Among their first concerns are, Can I be successful? How much money will I make? How will this affect my family? What will people think about my being in sales? Will there be enough business for me to be successful considering all of the other people selling the same products in my area? Will I have enough time? Is  this compatible with my family's time schedules? Can I do this while having another job or career? And on and on and on, just like the concerns you had when you first began. Now it becomes your job to answer these questions for your potential recruits and to relieve your prospects' fears. You also must anticipate the other problems and fears which may concern your prospects—you know what I mean, the ones they have not thought of yet.

Having had all of those thoughts in my first days in business, I taught myself the importance of positive self-talk. Do you use positive self-talk? Maybe you don't know what I mean when I say positive self-talk. It's more  of that "glass half-full" as opposed to the "glass half-empty" thinking which represents an outlook on life that you have the power to choose. It is really your choice. You decide whether you are an " I can do it" person or one of those "I can't do it," never-achieving folks. Being a "can-do" person myself, practically all of my own thoughts are about how I can succeed. No one ever achieved anything with an "I can't do it" start. When you put an "I can do it" attitude together with goal setting, then **you** have "positive self-talk" with results. "I can do it" thoughts lead to actions and actions lead to more success and satisfaction for you.

Think about the role model you can be for others when you overcome your fears and concerns and teach others the power of positive thinking. In our businesses, it is important to lead by example. If you want the members of your team to be top sellers and recruiters, you need to demonstrate the necessary qualities for others to follow your lead and achieve their own success. How rewarding that will be for both of you!

To be honest, I wasn't always a "positive self-talk" person. I was the kind of student who dreaded oral book reports, hoping the teacher would run out of time before he or she called on me for fear I wouldn't do well in my presentation. This lack of confidence continued for many years right up to the night that I decided to join the company I now represent. I decided I would conduct my network marketing business by taking catalog orders only. That way, I would avoid public speaking—I would only have to speak with one or two people at a time.

The night my recruiter came to speak with Jim and me about my joining her company, she said just doing catalog orders would not be a very successful way to build my business. She told us that I really would have to do presentations to groups of people to be successful. That was enough to scare me—having to talk to groups of people convinced me this was not the business for me. I wasn't about to torment myself doing oral presentations. Well, as I was thinking that, Jim, being the supportive husband, blurted out, "I'll get the check book for the deposit." I don't know why (I am not a violent person.), but I just kicked him under the table. He said very indiscreetly, "Why did you just kick me?" I had to quickly make a decision between admitting my fear or starting a new business. I decided to just sign up. We handed her the deposit for my kit.

Now I was committed. I spent the night lying awake trying to convince myself that I was going to make this work. "I will not fail," I kept telling myself; I did not want to disappoint Jim after the confidence he had just demonstrated in me. Gradually, the scary thoughts became positive self-talk about how I could meet this new challenge and I was on my way to a new career.

Chapter 6

Why Sales?

Chapter 6

Why Sales?

Long before I got into sales, my friends and family members told me that my personality was such that I would make a great salesperson. I didn't understand why so many of them suggested selling to me as a career. (Maybe it was the fact that I was the number one Girl Scout cookie seller in my fourth grade troop that made them think I was cut out for sales.) But, as I said before, they turned out to be right.

I never really knew why selling was not appealing to me. Maybe it was some experience hidden deep in my subconscious that I had with some terribly over-zealous, insistent and pushy  salesperson. We have all met that kind of person. Why is it that those obnoxious types stick out in our minds? What about those many wonderful salespeople who actually made our shopping experiences so much easier and pleasant that we really found ourselves enjoying the process? We have all had those pleasant shopping days many

73

more times than we have had unpleasant ones.

Let's talk about the kind of salesperson who gave us those pleasant experiences and what they did that made them successful salespeople. When you are helping others, keep in mind that you want to be the kind of person you would want assisting you. In other words, you want your customer to go away with that same happy and satisfied feeling that you have experienced in the past. You know what I mean—the kind of salesperson that you seek out when you go back to that same store. A good salesperson cares about and thinks about what her or his customer wants or needs. When I go to the store, I want the person who helps me to think about what *I'm* looking for and what *my* needs are. I want her or his goal to be making my main interest her or his main interest. In other words, salespeople know that they earn their commission when I, as their customer, feel cared about, have come to trust their advice, and as a result, buy the product.

One of the most important ways you can demonstrate that you **care** for your customers is by asking them questions that will help you learn their wants and their needs and then truly **listening** to their answers. Remember that good listeners are not thinking about what to say next but are focusing on what they are hearing. You'll know you're helping your customers and asking the **right questions** when you begin to see them smiling and nodding in agreement with you. (You're watching your customers' reactions just like a lawyer watches a jury—to see if you are reaching them with your questions.) Then you will know you are "speaking their language" and that you are stimulating their thoughts about the products and services you have to offer.

It was just that type of *sharing and caring* person that changed my feelings about my being in sales; that salesperson was just as professional as a lawyer, teacher, or doctor. We are all here to help others in a professional way, each profession requiring its own set of skills and knowledge. My father, a lawyer, has often said he also is a salesman; it's just that he sells facts instead of products. Don't forget that every major company has a marketing department—people we all think of as professionals. You too are in marketing. You are also a professional. You should always remember that.

After achieving the successes I have been fortunate to enjoy, I now understand what my friends and family meant when they said I would be great at sales. They knew I always wanted to be in a career where I was helping others through personal contact and contributing to their happiness. There was no doubt that I could achieve this result through sales while still being a stay-at-home mom. And, that's what they were **so** right about!

Let me share with you a personal experience that made me feel very good about sales. It made me realize that products really do not sell themselves, that it is confident, successful *salespeople* who make the sale by explaining the value and the usefulness of the product to their potential customer. The salesperson's description of the product's features and benefits is based upon the information that she or he gathers from the customer, through the asking of questions. Then the salesperson can easily determine which product will meet her or his customer's needs.

Many years ago, shortly after starting my sales career, our refrigerator just died—not a good thing to happen with a limited budget and five children with big appetites. There just wasn't a repairperson with the magic fairy dust that could make the refrigerator well again. Jim and I faced the fact that we were suddenly in the market for a new appliance.

We took our two youngest children along with us on a mission to find the most affordable replacement available—keep in mind, it wasn't in our budget for that month. As we entered the appliance department of a nearby store and approached the refrigerator section, a salesperson met us and asked, "Can I help you?" This was the one and only question he ever asked. He didn't bother to gather any information about our budget, the size of our family, or how our family might make use of the fancy model that he was showing us. He didn't care enough to find out. But, he sure wanted to tell us which refrigerator we should buy—the most expensive one and, naturally, the one with the largest commission. We knew how buying that refrigerator would help *him* but we didn't know how it would help *us*. That was it— end of sale or rather **no** sale. We knew we couldn't possibly fit that refrigerator with all the extras into our budget. We said, "No thanks," and left the store.

At the second store, we were greeted by a very friendly salesperson. He asked, "What can I help you with today?" We told him we needed a new refrigerator, and he said, "I'll bet that wasn't in  your family budget this month. I'd like to ask you a few questions to get some information so that I can best help you." Although he saw two of our children, the salesperson was caring and smart enough not to assume he knew all about our family. When he asked about the size of our family, we told him that we had three more children at home. He then asked, "Do your children drink enough water, or are they more interested in drinking sodas? Do they want to stop to get a drink every time they pass a water fountain? Do you think that it would be really helpful to have water available on the outside of your new refrigerator? And, they'd even get to push the button themselves—that's enticing to kids." He continued, "Do you find your older children are opening and closing the refrigerator all day to get ice for their drinks? Would it be helpful to have ice available on the outside too?" As we answered each of his many questions, I began to think he knew our family well.

We were ready to buy from him because of his attitude of *caring* enough about us to be sure that we got the right refrigerator that met our family's needs. He explained the refrigerator's functions and how those functions could be of great use to our family. He even made it possible for us to handle our budget problem. Know what? We actually bought the same refrigerator we were standing in front of in the first store where the guy could only say, "Can I help you?"

The second salesperson sure was helpful, and his helpfulness paid off for both of us. You know what he did? He *shared and cared.* Remember, up until *that* day I wondered whether being in sales was right for me. But, I realized how I could be helpful to others as a salesperson too after having met a truly professional salesperson who was so helpful to me. And by writing this book, I am reaching more people than I could ever hope to reach through personal contact and helping so many more. **I just love being in sales!**

We do need to recognize our business as our profession. Salespersons are needed for people to acquire anything—from buying a house to buying a car to, most importantly for us, purchasing the many different products we all have to offer. In addition, as I said before, isn't everyone in some form of sales? Doctors sell their capability to make us feel better. Concerning lawyers, Honest Abe Lincoln said, "A lawyer's time and advice is his stock in trade." Now if that's not a statement about selling, nothing is! And, teachers sell us every day on the value of what they are trying to teach—and even the value of homework!

I think you will agree we are all involved with people selling to us all the time. You know, when you think about it, ideas, yes, even ideas are sold. An idea that stays in someone's head is just a thought; but an idea that is "sold" to someone is placed in action and *then* it has meaning. Have an idea? Then you too must put it into action to be a successful salesperson.

What do you put into action? You put into action your ideas that are fueled by your expectations. Every successful businessperson has expectations or goals and for you to succeed, you too must have expectations. I think it's a good idea to write down your expectations. (This is a sound business practice that in the formal sense becomes part of what is called a business plan.) Then, you not only have something to remind you of your business objectives but something your "significant other" can see as well. In other words, this is another way to convince your "buddy" that you really are **in** business and not just enjoying a hobby.

Do not settle for what *just happens* to you in your business or even in your life. Unless you win the lottery or hit a slot machine jackpot, you are not likely to find success or satisfaction from chance events happening around you. It takes a plan, and with that plan, you can make it happen. We do have control over much of our lives, and it is up to us to take control whenever we can. Be clear on what the "ALL" is you want to achieve and determine what it will take for you to get there. Then (back to those expectations you've written down) add a plan to achieve those expectations, a plan as detailed as possible. When you're finished writing it out and you're satisfied with it, then decide you'll even do *better* than you ever thought possible, which will lead to results that are far above your own expectations. **And that's success.**

What expectations do you have for yourself in your business?

Do you settle for what happens or are you a "make it happen" business builder?

Chapter 7

Prospecting— Opening the Doors To New Opportunities

Chapter 7

Prospecting—Opening the Doors To New Opportunities

Every day we find ourselves in situations where we are talking to new people—in lines, on planes, at the park, and everywhere we go. Do you find yourself talking to people about the weather and other ice-breaking chitchat, wishing that you could just figure out a way to share what you do in your business? Here's good news—with just a few basic phrases and questions, you can be "out the door" prospecting in just a few minutes. Trust me, that's what I've done, and it works!

The skill we are working on right now is what I refer to as "bridging." Let's continue painting pictures. By "bridging," you are building a connection from a current thought to a new thought that is developed from the topic of conversation.

Are you ready to practice the skill of bridging? Remember practicing **is** doing. The good news is that the first time you approach someone to practice, you can actually get results. It's like learning to drive—the minute you are behind the wheel practicing, you are driving and moving forward while you are out there practicing. Let's start with some basic, prospecting language lessons.

Shopping Can Be Profitable

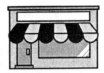

Did you ever realize shopping could lead to earning money? I have convinced Jim that shopping is important to the future of my business. That's right, Jim believes that the more I shop the more my business is growing. Seriously though, I am able to meet lots of potential recruits, hostesses, and customers on shopping trips.

Are you going to the mall or store today? While you are at the mall and standing in line at the register, you can be sharing information about your company with other customers in line with you. Here is how to start your conversation:

Doesn't the line seem really long today? (Or, short if that is the case.) *Do you shop here at this time often?*

After they respond, say:

I'm really lucky that I have my own home-based business and I can really choose when I want to shop here. This certainly seems to be a bad time (or good time if the line is short). Have you ever heard of (your company)? I'm always looking for people to join my sales team. Have you ever thought about doing something alongside your family and all your other activities?

Whether their answer here is yes or no, you can continue sharing, if you find the person to whom you're speaking receptive to your conversation.

(Your company) is a lot of fun. I would love to get some information to you about all the services we offer. Would you feel comfortable giving me your name and telephone number so that I can do that?

Be prepared with a small notepad, pen, and business cards.

You can say the same thing to the next person. Do you notice a pattern? Icebreaker questions, such as "Do you come here often?" or "Does the line seem long?" (Or short, whichever the case may be.), are questions that can work in any situation, whether you are at the zoo, in a restaurant, at a park, or in line at the grocery store. The key to success is the *sharing*, and the follow-up is the *caring* which is equally important to your success.

Sharing in the Parking Lot

Do you find yourself in a parking lot getting in or out of your car at the same time people are getting in or out of a car near yours? Don't hesitate to say:

Do you live in this area?

If they say yes, say:

*Great! I was wondering if you could share some information with others in your neighborhood. (**Your company**) is expanding and we could really use some help. I'm always looking for people to join me. Have you ever thought about doing something **alongside** your family and all your other activities? This business is a lot of fun. I'd love to get some information to* *you about all the services we offer. Would you feel comfortable giving me your name and telephone number so that I can do that?*

If they seem hesitant to give you their name and phone number but they look like a good prospect, offer them your business card and invite them to call you for more information.

If they say they do not live in this area, just ask where they're from. Then proceed to say:

*I was wondering if you could share some information with others where you live. (**Your company**) is expanding and we could really use some help. Have you ever thought about doing something **alongside** your family and all your other activities? I'm always looking for people to join me. This business is a lot of fun, and I'd love to get some information to you about all the services we offer. Would you feel comfortable giving me your name and telephone number so that I can do that?*

89

The Person You Meet Today Could Be a Star on Your Team Tomorrow

There are many other situations when you will be talking to people such as at the mall, post office, bank, and other stops in your daily routine. This time you will be inviting the people who are helping you to consider becoming a part of your team. The invitation will really make people to whom you speak feel especially good because you are paying them a compliment about their "people skills."

Throughout your daily routine, make a point to talk to people you see doing a great job assisting you, and say:

I noticed how great you are with your customers. Have you worked here long?

After they respond, then say:

*I love working with people, too. I have my own home-based business. Have you heard of (**your company**)? I'm always looking for people to join my sales team. Have you ever thought about doing something **alongside*** *your family and all your other activities to earn extra income? This business is a lot of fun. I'd love to get some information to you about all the services we offer.*

Then proceed to share your business card and say:

Would you feel comfortable giving me your name and telephone number so that I can do that?

One very good place to have some of your business cards available is in your wallet. Every time you hand someone money, your card will remind you that by *sharing and caring* you can give the people you are meeting an **OPPORTUNITY!** You may want to keep a few extra cards in your wallet so that you can hand one over to the cashier. Remember that you are rewarded financially for giving other people an opportunity.

At Your Next Appointment Someone Could Be Waiting to Be Invited to Join You

Are you going to a doctor's appointment,

dental appointment, beauty shop, or barbershop? The first thing to remember is to share information with the receptionist. After signing in, ask the receptionist if she or he could share some information with her or his fellow employees. Just say:

> *Could you please share this information with your co-workers?*

Now is the time to leave a catalog with a label on it saying, "HELP WANTED. (**YOUR COMPANY**) is expanding in this area. This is an office copy. Please call me at (your telephone number) for your personal catalog." Don't forget to personally invite the receptionist to join you. You can say:

> *I really appreciate your sharing this. Have you ever thought about doing something fun **alongside** what you are doing now to earn some extra income for your family?*

Be prepared! Have information at all times. Spend an evening preparing prospecting packets while watching TV. (Better yet, since this is a home-based business where everybody benefits, why not enlist the assistance of your husband or

92

older children and ask them to prepare your prospecting packets for you?) Include a business card, information about your products, and information about your career opportunity. It is a good idea to have packets in the car, so if the time seems right *and* you have the person's phone number, you can offer to go get some information from the car.

Child Care Providers Could Enjoy Being Paid to Work with Adults Too

Do you have children in childcare or do you know anyone who works in day care? Child care providers and others, such as tutors and music teachers, really enjoy a chance to be out with adults, and through your business you give them the opportunity to not only have adult contact but to earn money at the same time. Check your local papers and grocery store bulletin boards for phone numbers of people doing in-home child care or any other activities from home. Call them and say:

I found your name in the paper. I do not need childcare (or whatever service they are offering). I am calling today because I also have a home-based business and wanted to know if you are familiar with (your

93

*company). I am looking for people who enjoy working from home to join me. Have you ever thought of doing something **alongside** your childcare business and family activities? Would you enjoy being able to get out in the evenings and be paid to be with adults, sharing our products?*

Keep track of all the telephone numbers you'll be accumulating in a file box or on your computer so you won't call the same ones over and over.

Traveling Can Be
A Prospecting Trip

Are you traveling by train or plane? While you are waiting at the airport or train station, look for a seat by friendly-looking people. Ask them if they are going on a trip or waiting for someone to arrive. Remember you can ask questions like:

Do you travel often?

Or, you could say

Are you going on a vacation or traveling for work?

Then lead into your *sharing* part of the conversation and say:

I was wondering if you could share some information with others where you live. (Your company) is expanding and we could really use some help. Have you ever thought about doing something alongside your family and all your other activities? I'm always looking for people to join me. This business is a lot of fun. I'd love to get some information to you about all the services we offer. Would you feel comfortable giving me your name and telephone number so I can do that?

Are you traveling by car? Take advantage of the stops you make along the way to share information with anyone, everywhere. Ask people in restaurants, hotels, tollbooths, rest stops, and other similar places if they could share information by saying:

I'm a representative with (your company) and I'm visiting in this area. I was

*wondering if you could share some
information with others where you live.
(**Your company**) is expanding and we could
really use some help. Have you ever
thought about doing something **alongside**
your family and all your other activities?
I'm always looking for people to join me.
This business is a lot of fun. I'd love to get
some information to you about all the
services we offer. Would you feel
comfortable giving me your name and
telephone number so that I can do that?*

 **Are you beginning to recognize the Ilene
Meckley prospecting-language pattern?**

Prospecting at the Same Time
You Are Enjoying a Good Meal!

Are you going to a restaurant today? Have
you ever met wait staff who gave you fantastic
service and had great people skills? Be sure to tell
them how much you enjoyed being at their table.
Then say:

*I am looking for people just like you to work
with me in my business. Have you ever
heard of (**your company**)? Would earning*

*extra income by doing something **alongside** your current job be of interest to you? I'm always looking for people to join me. This business is a lot of fun. I'd love to get some information to you about all the services we offer. Would you feel comfortable giving me your name and telephone number so that I can do that?*

Special Events for Prospecting in Your Community

A good way to meet people in your neighborhood or in a new community is to set up a display of your products at a county fair, or a church or synagogue bazaar. Read through community newspapers and look for additional events such as spaghetti suppers, PTA fundraisers, or meetings where you could be a speaker about your home-based business. At these events you should be sure people see a sign letting them know you are looking for people to join you.

Ask each person who walks up to your display if she or he is familiar with your company. This is the time that it is important to share current information about your products with others **AND** tell them that you are looking for people to join you in your business. Remember it's important to hand **everyone** something with your name on it saying you have an income-earning opportunity for her or him. As you hand the material to her or him (keep in mind that she/he didn't stop by your booth looking for a business), be sure you extend a personal invitation to take advantage of all of your services with a very special technique. This is often referred to as the "Fishing for Whales" theory. Why go for the small fish first? Here's the way it should be:

Offer the opportunity to join you and become a part of your company.

As she/he is looking at your products, say:

*Have you ever heard of (**your company**) before seeing them here today? We are here today to be sure that people are aware of our products and to also let you know that we are expanding and could really use more* *representatives. Would earning extra income by doing something **alongside** your current job be of interest to you? I'm always looking for people to join me. This business is a lot of fun.*

Was the answer no? Then:

Offer the opportunity to be a hostess and to receive free products.

*I would love to help you get some of our products for **FREE**. Is there a time in the next week or two I could come show the products to you and your friends? As a "thank you," you can earn lots of free products. What do you think, can we set a date?*

Did you still get a no? Well then, go on to our "small fish" offer:

Offer the opportunity to purchase your **products** or place an order. You could also offer to stop by for a personal shopping appointment.

> *I'd still love for you to be able to see our products. Is there a time in the next few days that I can pop by and show you some of our current products?*

In addition to looking in the newspaper for community events at which you can do some "fishing," you can be pro-active; you can call schools, organizations, churches and synagogues to see if they will be sponsoring a fair or bazaar. Don't forget to also share information with the person to whom you speak. Just say:

> *Have you ever heard of (**your company**)? Would earning extra income doing something **alongside** your current job be of interest to you? I'm always looking for people to join me. This business is a lot of fun. I'd love to get some information to **you** about all the services we offer. Would you feel comfortable giving me your home telephone number so that I can do that?*

Still Prospecting?
Did You Ever Realize
How Many Places
You Could *Share and Care?*

Are you doing a workshop (presentation, party, demonstration, or any other type of selling event)? In these activities you are actually **earning income** while prospecting. At the same time that you are helping your hostess earn the most, free products that she can, you are meeting potential representatives and hostesses. It is really important that *during your introduction* you begin to paint pictures of what your company has to offer—from the career opportunity to the hostess benefits to the value of your products. Be sure to share your personal story and include why other people have decided to become a part of your company. Here's what *I* say:

> *I want to thank Mary for inviting me here tonight and thank you for taking the time to be here. Thirteen years ago, I started my home-based business with Discovery Toys, Inc. I had been a working mom outside the home and was very unhappy leaving my five young children at home. I made a sudden decision to quit my job, forgetting that my bills would still keep coming. My husband,*

Jim, was very supportive about my quitting work; yet we still felt my missing income would be a challenge. Thanks to Discovery Toys, Inc., that problem didn't last for long.

*I'm so glad that my earlier fear of speaking in front of groups didn't keep me from starting and building my business. My family has had amazing travel experiences we would never have had without my business. I hope tonight, after hearing me talk about the products, that you too will think about the benefits that you could have for your family. If some extra income, personal growth, or travel sound appealing to you, then definitely talk to me tonight about how you could do this business **alongside** your family and other activities.*

Don't forget to personally invite people to join you, host a selling event, or be one of your valued customers. It is important to send them home with a flyer advertising your career opportunities. Suggest that they share it with a friend after taking a look at it themselves. Again, keep in mind they didn't attend the event looking for a business, although we hope we've planted the seed that will now have them going home thinking about starting a business.

An important thing to do after your selling event is what some of us refer to as Big MAC or Big WAC calls. A Big MAC call is a "Morning After the presentation Call." (A Big WAC is a "Week After the presentation Call." Try not to make it a Big YAC call—a Year After Call!) Throughout your presentation you should make mental notes of the comments of your hostess and her guests (and *written* notes as soon as you can). Then, when you call the next morning to thank them for hosting or attending the presentation, you can also bridge into asking them to join you in your company. For example, if you overheard a guest say she would love to order more of your products, but she doesn't have the money right now, you could say:

> *I was so glad you came to Mary's party last night. Thank you for coming. I want to be sure that you have my phone number in your address book in case I can ever be any help to you in the future. I was wondering have you had a chance to look at the information that I gave you last night? I hope you'll consider giving (**your company**) a try as a representative or hostess. Is there any additional information you would like at this time concerning joining me or being a hostess?*

Remember—always start by asking if they would consider joining you as a representative (fishing for the whale). No bites? Then try for a selling event (big fish). If still no bites, since they have just made a purchase, ask them if they would like to be contacted in the future with information about new products (little fish). Don't forget to ask for a referral to someone who was unable to attend the presentation. You can say:

> *Do you know anyone who was unable to attend last night, or someone the hostess might not have even known such as a friend of yours, who I could call and check with to see if they are familiar with (**your company**) and if they would know how to reach a representative?*

Advertising

Do you invite incoming callers to join you in your business? Have you ever received an incoming call from a telemarketer who just sounded so pleasant that you thought she/he would be great in your business? Try saying the following:

*I was wondering if you own the business that you are calling about. You are so pleasant on the phone; I think you would be great having your own business. Have you ever heard of (**your company**)? Have you ever thought about doing something alongside your family and all your other activities? I imagine that now is not a good time to discuss our business; would you feel comfortable giving me your name and telephone number so that I can share some additional information with you?*

Are you advertising your business? When I receive a call in response to my ad, I like to ask the caller:

What attracted you to my ad?

In that way I can find out what features and benefits of the business I need to tell them about first. I don't want to waste their time or mine talking about things they do not want to hear. In addition, I always ask them:

*Is there anyone else you know who might also like to hear about (**your company**)?*

When running an ad, remember it's just one way to prospect. Don't expect that the ad will always give you results. When you start advertising, you need to be comfortable with the fact that not all advertising brings immediate results. Often advertising has a cumulative effect. Advertising is one good way, though, to meet potential representatives, hostesses, and customers.

It is important, in the beginning of your career, to try to meet face to face with those who respond to your ads. After you gain more experience, you may find that a lot of the recruiting interview and qualifying can be done over the phone. A good question to ask potential representatives to determine whether you should meet with them and whether or not your time would be well spent is:

*If you like the products and I can show you how this business can fit **alongside** your family and other activities, would you be ready to get started?*

****

Play the Alphabet
Scavenger Hunt Game

Do you want some new leads? Do you wonder whom you can call to share your business? You never have to wonder whom to call if you always remember to ask everyone for referrals. The Alphabet Scavenger Hunt Game is a fun way to ask for referrals **and** to jog your memory concerning people you know you can call.

For example, think of all the people you know whose name begins with the letter A. Think of all the people you know who live in a state or city that starts with the letter A. Think of all the people you know who have an occupation, hobby, or sport that they play that starts with the letter A. Think of a place that starts with the letter A where you can share your business.

Call customers, friends, and family and tell them you are on a scavenger hunt for your business. Say:

I hope you can help me with my scavenger hunt. Today I'm trying to meet some new people to see if they have heard of (your company). I'm on the letter A. Can you think of some people whose names start with the letter A, live in a city or state that starts with A, or have a profession that starts with A? The purpose of my call to them will be to make sure they know someone who represents our company so that they can take advantage of our services too.

Here are a few suggestions to get you started:

For A: aunts, accountants, attorneys, Alaska, Alabama, Arizona, Arkansas, Atlanta, Albuquerque, alumni, ambitious people.

Already exhausted all the As? Go on to the next letter in the alphabet.

For B: bakers, baseball players, beauticians, biologists, businesspersons, Boston, Buffalo, Baltimore.

For C: clergymen, child care providers, cooks, consultants, chiropractors, coaches, counselors, church members, California, Colorado,

Connecticut, Chicago, Cleveland, Chattanooga, Cincinnati, Christmas card lists.

For D: doctors, dentists, delivery people, drivers, doers, Denver, Delaware.

For E: everyone, engineers, enthusiastic people, extra curricular activities, electricians.

For F: florists, fire fighters, fun-loving people, Florida, friends, family.

For G: government workers, go-getters, Georgia, Gainesville, Georgetown.

For H: healthcare workers, hospital workers, Hawaii, Houston, Hanover, Harrisburg, health clubs.

For I: insurance salespeople, inventors, Indiana, Illinois, Idaho, Iowa.

For J: judges, journalists, Jamestown, Juneau, Johnson City, Jacksonville.

For K: karate instructors, kennel workers, Kansas, Kentucky.

For L: landscapers, librarians, Lincoln, Las Vegas, Louisiana, libraries.

For M: manicurists, musicians, Michigan, Maine, Montana, Massachusetts, Maryland, malls, museums, movie theaters.

For N: Nevada, New York, New Mexico, Nebraska, nurses, newspaper workers, neighbors.

For O: orthodontists, orthopedists, Oregon, Oklahoma, Ohio, opera singers.

For P: pediatricians, photographers, painters, Pittsburgh, Phoenix, Pennsylvania, parents.

For Q: quilters, Queens (New Yorkers, of course, not royalty, although if you know them why not ask them for a referral?).

For R: real estate agents, researchers, retirees, Rochester, Racine.

For S: sculptors, secretaries, swimming instructors, Sarasota, San Antonio, San Diego, San Francisco, Sacramento.

For T: taxidermists, tailors, tour directors, Tacoma, Tucson, Texas.

For U: university instructors, utility workers, Utah.

For V: veterinarians, voice teachers, Virginia.

For W: waiters, wedding consultants, widows, Walla Walla, Waxahachie, West Virginia.

For X: x-ray technicians, xylophonists.

For Y: yacht brokers, yoga instructors, Yuma.

For Z: zoologists, Zanzibar.

Okay, that last one is a bit of a stretch (although you just might be able to get a monopoly in Zanzibar) but you get the idea, don't you? In addition, remember that you are asking the people you contact to help you with this Alphabet Scavenger Hunt, as well as jogging your *own* memory. So, get started *sharing.*

Need even more names to call? Start doing what I refer to as information calls. There are so many people who would not know how to find any of us in the companies we represent. It's up to us to get the word out about our career opportunity and our products. So, if you've run out of names to call, bring out the phone book! From the phone book call and say:

Hi! My name is ____ and I live in the area. I am calling you today to meet some people to share information about what I do. This is not a sales call but an opportunity for me to tell others about my business so that when you do need my services, you will know how to reach me. Is this a good time to take just a couple of minutes of your time?

If the person you have called says yes, then say:

*Thanks so much. As I mentioned before, my name is ____ and I am a representative with (**your company**). Have you ever heard of us?*

If she says no, then just continue to share some more information:

*We offer three services that I'd love to share with you. One is that I am really excited about my business and we are always looking for people to join us sharing (**your company**).*

Then just ask:

*Have you ever thought about doing something **alongside** your family and other activities to earn extra income, or would you enjoy doing something to help others?*

If she says, "No, I, don't think I'm really interested in doing something like that," say:

The second service we offer is an opportunity to see our products when you host a party, and as a thank you, we have a generous hostess plan. You can earn lots of our products for free. Is there a time in the next two weeks we could set a date for a presentation?

If she says no to that question, then offer to do a personal shopping appointment, so she or he can still see the products.

Is there a time when I could just pop by and show you some of our products?

If she says **no** to that question and she seems friendly, ask her if she can think of anyone she knows whom you could call to see if that person has heard of your company and would know where to find us if she needed our services.

If she says **no** to that question, ask her if there is a time she would like you to check back with her. If she says yes, great! If she says no, that's okay because someone else will need your services. It is just your job to find who they are.

If I haven't convinced you yet that "just asking" is very important to you in your business, and to life in general, there's one very special story I would like to share about my son, David.

David wanted to go to a very small, very expensive private college. We told our children we wanted to help them with their education, but with five children, we expected them to attend one of our fine state colleges or universities. We told David that we would give him the amount of the state tuition, but he would have to have enough in scholarships or grants to make up the difference.

David had a 4.3 average in high school, and we were very hopeful that he would get his wish. Fortunately, he was offered a scholarship from the school of his choice; unfortunately, it was not enough to make up the difference. David, being determined, said to Jim and me, "I just have to ask the college for a bigger scholarship." I was so nervous when he made the call to "just ask." After his call, we all anxiously awaited the college's response to his request.

A few days later I received a call from the college when David wasn't home. The person calling asked if I had seen the essay that David wrote when he applied. She told me that the scholarship committee had met, at which time she read David's essay to the members. She said,

"When they heard the paragraph about his mother telling him to never give up and to always be confident, to 'just ask' for the things he wants and never settle for less, we decided that we didn't want his mother to be wrong." So, the exciting news is that David is attending the college of his choice with a **full** tuition scholarship. Just think how different his life would be if he had not "just asked." Remember, if you don't ask, it's an automatic **no** and nothing really changes. If you "just ask," you could get a yes, and everything changes.

One of the most important pieces of advice I can give you about prospecting is to decide right now that the object of your effort is to *share and care.* You know you will have succeeded when, at the end of the day, you are pleased with the amount of information you have shared. Don't measure your success by how you are doing in short periods of time. Your success is not based upon your convincing everyone you meet to join you in your business the first time you mention it to her, or even the second time. Rather, it is all about your planting seeds and helping those people who are interested in what you have to offer feel confident that, based upon the information you have provided, they are making the right decision to join you. That's what *sharing and caring* is really all about.

Chapter 8

The Language of Recruiting (or Ilene's Steps to Success)

Chapter 8

The Language of Recruiting (or Ilene's Steps to Success)

What can you do to turn your "prospecting" leads into members of your team? Recruiting is the magic word! Be **proud** that you are a recruiter for your company.

I have always loved the *action* of recruiting, but I did not like the *word* recruiting. It reminded me of joining the armed services, not joining a network marketing company. Then one day, while traveling, I met a woman who changed my feelings by helping me see how special the **word** recruiting really is.

While sitting next to her on a plane, and trying to distract myself during take-off, I asked her whether she was traveling for business or pleasure (a good way to start a conversation while traveling). When she replied that she was on a business trip, I asked, "What kind of work do you do?" She proudly answered, "I am a recruiter!"

I thought, "Great! I'm going to hear all about the army." (Let's face it, before the days when I really understood the word recruiting, I didn't know enough to think about the real *meaning* of the word.) I then asked my fellow passenger whom she recruits. She replied, "I have such a special job. I find great bands and entertainers to perform at weddings, bar mitzvahs, and the like to help create memories for a lifetime."

Then she asked me what I do. I told her, taking a deep breath and using "that" word for the very first time, "I'm a recruiter, too!" She asked me whom *I* recruited. I replied, "I look for people who would like the chance to be able to have their own business where they're more in control of their lives and paychecks. I really give people an opportunity to do things they may have never been able to do." She then said, "Wow, we really have special jobs, don't we?" And that we do!

Have you ever had the experience of being recruited by someone outside of your business? How did it feel? Think about all the instances when someone is so thrilled to hear from a recruiter. For example, there is the high school senior anxiously waiting to hear from college recruiters. The child who has auditioned for the school play, football team, church choir or the like is eagerly waiting for the phone to ring or to see his or her name posted on the list, representing the fact that he or she made it and had been recruited!

Just think, someone may have tried to recruit *you* recently—has anyone said what a great pie you make, and asked you to bring one to Thanksgiving dinner or to the PTA bake sale? That's recruiting, too. When someone compliments you on your talents and capabilities, asking you to *use* those special skills to be a part of something; **that's what is behind the word RECRUITING!** And that's what *sharing and caring* is all about—helping people realize they too have very special skills that would fit perfectly into your business.

What thoughts come to **your** mind when you hear the word recruiting, good ones or bad ones? You now know that I feel the word recruiting equals *sharing and caring,* a very positive thought.

For those of you who are not totally convinced that recruiting is positive, look at the words below and compare the connotations based upon the words that come to your mind when you hear that word recruiting. Substitute the positive word for the negative word and watch how your thoughts also become positive.

Negative	*or*	Positive
Pushy	*or*	Encouraging
Nosy	*or*	Caring
Talking "at" people	*or*	Asking questions
Manipulative	*or*	Informative
Convincing	*or*	Inviting
Ambivalent	*or*	Unsure
Fear	*or*	Lacks confidence
Not now	*or*	In the future

I firmly believe that when you know the language of prospecting and recruiting, you can feel confident when you are talking to anyone, anywhere. By using carefully chosen words and phrases, you will begin to speak the language of recruiting. Just like learning any other language, you will start out with a few basic, positive words that will develop into positive sentences and then you will be able to share your own experiences, just as I have shared with you. The key is practice, practice, practice.

Aren't we lucky that we do not have to wait for our customers to come to our store? There are people we meet everywhere who can become our customers and next recruits. Our job is to share the benefits that we have to offer. Then we need to be able to help the prospect feel confident in giving what we offer a try.

Now what do you do with all of those prospecting leads you acquired from the skills you learned in the last chapter? You need to follow up with phone calls. By making a minimum of ten phone contacts a day, five days a week, you will have fifty contacts in one week. At the end of four weeks, you will have made two hundred contacts— just doing only ten calls a day.

You may call over ten people before you get a positive response. Then you may get several positive responses in a row. It really doesn't matter; you can't sell or recruit without making telephone contacts, so keep on calling. By the time you have completed the 200 calls you should have a very pleasant mix of new customers, new hostesses and new recruits. Don't forget that number 200 may become a top national sales leader on your team, and you will be very glad you didn't stop at number 199.

I share this with you to help you understand that the contacts you are making, even when the contact sometimes results in a no, will still lead you to those yeses for which you are working so hard. Selling and recruiting is a sorting process, and every contact you make, whether a yes or no, is necessary for you to reach your goal. Remember that in order to have a successful telephone call, you must help the person you contacted feel good about you, your products, and your company. It is then that she or he may come to a decision that she or he wishes to either buy your products, become a host or hostess or, best of all, become a member of your team.

Are you an effective communicator? Do people get excited when you share your passion for your business? Are you able to paint pictures when you talk to others? Can you paint a picture with words about why your business makes you so happy? Does the person to whom you're speaking come away thinking, "Wow, she really loves her business"? Here's what you can say:

> *I really love working for a company that sells wonderful products that I am excited to share with my customers. I also love that I am able to work at home and be here for my family when they need me. Have you ever thought about doing something **alongside** your family and other activities to earn additional income?*

The following scripts **work!** (**Trust me!**) Read them over and over, and practice them (with your husband, your mother, your best friend—or into your tape recorder if no one else is around to help). Practice them until *my* words become *your own words*. When that happens, you will never again have to think, "What do I say?" Instead, you'll think, "What would Ilene say?" The right words will come with ease.

You may be wondering why I want you to use **my** words. Let me illustrate. Suppose you decided to take a French course so that you can communicate with a friend who just arrived in this country from France and who doesn't speak a word of English. At your last French class, you learned to say the words "rose" and "flower." Now, being very excited about your new language skills, you rush to tell your new friend (in French of course) that you really love *red roses.* Suppose instead that you mistakenly tell her that you really love *flowers.* Your friend shares with your husband that you really love flowers, and, being the thoughtful spouse that he is, he surprises you with a bouquet of *pink carnations.* Has your communication been effective? Obviously not, something was lost in the translation. Don't make the same mistake in the language of recruiting. I *can* tell you that my words *do* work!

Whenever you ask someone to join you and she replies, "Yes, but...." It generally means that she lacks confidence in some area such as having the time, the skill, or whatever. Perhaps she believes that she is too shy or she may even lack familiarity with how network marketing really works. The fact that she said yes indicates a desire to join you, and now you have to deal with the "but" part of her statement. This means you have to ask the appropriate questions to discover the actual reason for the hesitation, and when possible, you can alleviate her concerns.

Often by responding to your questions, the potential representative hearing her own answers can reach a comfortable decision. Don't just talk **at** the person you are inviting to join you; we do not want her to feel pushed into a decision. Provide enough information to help her conclude that she wants to try out the business, host a selling event, or perhaps just buy your products. We are the ones who know the "why's," and it is our job to help the people we are talking to become interested in the "why's."

Here is another picture I'd like to paint to help you understand how that is done. Have you ever had a friend sit down at a restaurant and say, "I'll just have coffee. I'm really not hungry." When the food comes to the table, suddenly she says, "That looks delicious" or "That smells so good." You offer her a taste, and then she decides to order. Did she really become hungry suddenly, or did the way the food looked, smelled, or tasted cause her to decide to order?

That's really what we do with our prospecting. We are letting the prospect "see, smell, and taste" our products so that she may be tempted to try us out. We have to find out what it is that would tempt each individual to try us out. Then we have to be able to address her concerns and handle any doubts or lack of confidence through our questions and her answers.

Do you remember my refrigerator story? Was I looking for the kind of refrigerator I purchased, or did the questions the second salesperson asked whet my appetite? Then I decided to "taste a bite" and he got the sale. What he did through his questions was create the desire in me for his product that I needed. I never felt "pushed," only fortunate that he knew how to ask questions to help me choose what would be the best product for me.

Let's get to the "how to" of recruiting.

What does it mean when someone says, "I would like to join you, but...?" Let's look at some possible meanings of what the potential representative is saying, and the questions you can ask in response. First, let her know how you feel:

I really feel a home-based business can fit into any lifestyle. I know a lot of people feel they need to wait for the right time. What would make it the right time for you to join me?

Then no matter what she says, ask:

May I share with you how many others have started businesses in the same situation? I really find that when we are waiting for a right time to come along, it just never seems to happen. Does that happen to you? What about job-testing, trying it out, to see how it works for you? Can I help you get started?

****

What do you ask, when your potential representatives say:

I'm too busy.

This really means, "Do I have enough time?" or " How am I going to find the time to meet people to be customers?"

In what types of activities are you involved?

Then say,

It sounds like you must know lots of people

from all of your activities. Do you think that they would be interested in (your company's) products?

Most of the time they will say yes. Then say:

That's great to hear! I would love to be sure they have a way to get our products too. Have you ever considered doing something alongside your family and other activities to earn extra income?

Whether they have previously considered it or not, the following question should be asked:

Would you enjoy being the one sharing our products and earning income at the same time?

If the answer is maybe or yes, then say:

That's great! So let's get you started. Who will be some of your first hostesses and new team members?

I could never sell anything.

This is really telling you they are uncomfortable with sales, lack confidence, and/or had a bad sales experience. Here is what you can say:

It sounds like you might have had a bad experience with someone in sales. Can you tell me about it?

After listening, ask:

Have you ever had an experience when making a purchase was so pleasant because of the salesperson?

After they reply say:

I felt funny about sales until I realized I could be the kind of salesperson that I would like helping me. I look at sales as helping people to feel comfortable about making a purchase. I am really proud of being in a profession where I can help people. Thinking about sales in that way, if I shared

some ideas with you to help you get started,
would you be interested in giving it a try?

If the potential recruit didn't have a bad
experience, but only appeared to lack confidence,
ask her to think about a situation when she had to
recruit people to bake cakes for a bake sale, get her
children to do their homework or pick up their toys.
Remind her that that is "selling," something we do
all the time.

****

I just moved here, and I don't know anyone.

They are probably thinking they won't have
any customers because they are feeling they can
only sell to friends and family. Here is what you
can say:

I am so glad we are talking. May I share
with you that you don't build a successful
business based on friends and family alone?
It can be a comfortable place to start, but
not knowing anyone now will not be a
problem. Would you like to know how you

could meet people who will become your customers, and some of them will even become your new friends too? Would some extra income be helpful to you when decorating your new home? I'd love for you to come meet some of my friends with whom I work, and you can meet some other new people in the area. Would you like to attend our next sales meeting on...? It would be great for you to "job test." What do you think about getting started?

****

I already work full time.

People are worried, "How can I do this while I have another job?" Again, let's be certain to reassure them by asking the right questions:

It would be great if you could be an on-site consultant.

(They may ask you, "What's that?")

An on-site consultant is someone who

services the people they work with, their own families, and others referred to them by their co-workers and family. Do you sometimes find yourself wishing you had time for shopping? Would it be a service to have an on-site consultant for (your company) right there at work?

Have you ever taken a class, known someone working on a graduate degree while working full time, or perhaps been on a PTA or church committee while working full time? What if you plan to treat a business the same way, planning what nights you can be available? What do you think? How about giving it a try?

****

I have a new baby (or I'm pregnant).

They are really trying to figure out how they can join you even though they have a new baby or are pregnant.

As a new parent, have you ever thought

*about doing something **alongside** your new family to earn extra income?*

If a new mom is saying she misses the adults from work and wishes she had time for herself, then personalize it and say:

Would being able to go out a couple nights a week sound appealing to you? You could actually be paid to be with adults. What do you think?

When someone is pregnant or just had a baby, another question to ask is:

Have you ever thought about trying a home-based business now and testing it out so that you can decide whether or not working from home would be a good career choice for you?

Another great comment to make is:

I have really enjoyed networking with the other parents that are my customers. You can get a lot of great ideas such as learning how to get stains out or how to potty train your children just by listening to conversations at the parties. Would it be fun and helpful to you to meet a lot of new parents?

****

I'll be moving soon.

People who are moving may be thinking, "Why start a business when I am so busy?" They may also have the same thoughts as a person who just moved there, "Whom will I know?" Our job again is to help them gain the confidence that they can start a new business by joining us even while they are dealing with the move. Say:

Moving can be a great time to start your business. Will you be getting your kids and yourself involved in new activities, organizations, a church, or a synagogue? I think you will agree that when you meet someone for the first time the question of what you do often comes up. Can you see how easy it will be to introduce your business to all the new people you are meeting? Will you be seeing a lot of people in the next few weeks before you move? You can develop a customer base where you live now before your move and one where you are moving. May I share how others have been very successful starting a business while in the process of moving?

****

The kids are just going back to school.

We need to help people realize that there will always be things going on in their lives, and that's why it is so important to use the word **alongside**. Ask them what kinds of things they will be doing while the kids are going back to school, or whatever it is they are busy doing (getting ready for holidays or such). Then say:

*It sounds like you will be busy and you will be in contact with lots of people. This is a great time to start your business. May I share with you how you could be starting your business right **alongside** getting the kids back to school? What do you think?*

I have to check with my husband.

This can mean a number of things. Unfortunately, it may be a way to put off having to say no to you, or it could mean that she and her husband make joint decisions. It is important to prepare the potential recruit with answers to questions her spouse may have. To get a feel for how a spouse will feel about a business you need to say:

> *I certainly respect that. Would your spouse mind if you were going to take an aerobics class a couple nights a month?*

If she says no, say:

> *That's great! How do you think he would feel if you spent the same amount of time doing presentations for your new business? What are some questions he might have? What would he like about your starting your own business? What concerns might he have?*

If the potential representative says her husband *would* mind the aerobics class, it probably means he does not want to parent alone or feels she needs to be at home for any other reason. We can't change their relationship. We can only ask:

Would it be helpful to have someone there to help with the kids while you do your selling events?

(Or)

Would you like some ideas to start your business by working during the day?

Again, you can encourage her by asking:

Would you like to be able to work this out so you can give it try?

If she is truly not interested, she will say no.

****

There are already too many people selling in my area.

It sounds like they are worried that there is not enough business to go around. They need reassurance that there are plenty of customers for their business. Say:

> *It sounds like you know a lot of people already doing this. That's great; I always like to know and meet other representatives. Whom do you know doing this?*

Nine times out of ten, they hardly know anyone. If they give you a lot of names, ask how they know them. You should inquire if they are involved in other activities so they can introduce the products to families there. Point out that even by doing three events a week, they would only need 12 hostesses in a month. (Wouldn't we be thrilled with a representative who regularly did 12 events per month?) Then ask:

> *What is the population of your town? If you divided the population by the number of representatives in (your company), you would have ____ potential hostesses and customers per representative.*

140

Another good thing to ask them is, "When were you last invited to a party?"

****

I have too many kids.

Again this can be an excuse, or they could be concerned about time. Share your experiences about the people you have met who have several children. You are welcome to share my story. Ask them if they would like to know how others do it with a large family. Again, encourage them by saying:

> *I think you will find that having a large family you are usually involved with lots of other people who are likely customers. Do you think that they would be interested in our products? It would be great for you to "job test" and give it a try. What do you think about trying for just eight weeks?*

****

141

I'm a single parent.

They are concerned with time and who will watch the children. Remember that they might have a support system. Ask them:

Do you have local friends or family members in the area to support you in a new business?

(OR)

Do you know another single mom who might be interested in working with you and sharing the childcare for each of your children? What do you think?

****

I'm shy; I don't feel comfortable approaching people.

I can certainly relate to this one, and if you do too, tell them that. If this has not been a problem for you, borrow *my* story. Ask them if this is something they would like to overcome. Reassure them that there have been many people who have found that network marketing is a good way to experience personal growth. If they still feel uncomfortable, ask them:

Would you like your kids to grow up feeling more comfortable?

When they say yes, be sure to let them know the best way that they can have that happen is to work on it themselves.

****

My husband travels frequently because of his work.

It is often hard to find a job that works around a spouse's travel schedule. Start the conversation by asking:

Does he usually know his schedule a couple of weeks in advance? Do you think you would enjoy having something flexible that works around his traveling? Would a business like this be helpful to add some income to your family?

Or, you could say:

Do you know others with spouses in similar situations where you could help each other out with the kids when either one or both of the spouses are traveling? May I share with you some ways that people in your situation have been very successful? What do you think about giving it a try?

****

This is just not the right time.

This indicates that she feels something has to "give" in order to join you. Perhaps she is having serious health problems or a family member is very ill. That's the time to leave the door open and say:

I really want you to feel good about joining me. What would make it the right time?

144

I asked this question to a potential representative once and her answer was next week when her mother-in-law was going home. You need to ask follow-up questions to find out what your potential representative means when they say something like it's not the right time.

****

I'm just not interested.

Sometimes people say, "I'm just not interested." At times the potential recruit's body language may communicate a lack of interest. Trying to recruit her then is like trying to help a child who says, "I'm bored"—anything you suggest they just do not want to hear! This can mean one of two things. It may be that they are just not interested *right now*, or it may be that they will *never* be interested. So, keep the door open with a question like this:

From time to time, our company sends us updated information on our product line and business opportunities. Would you like me to keep you informed in case something changes in your life?

Sometimes you just have to ask the question, "Are you having trouble saying no to me?" If that is the case, by asking this question, you will help people feel comfortable giving you a no. However, they may say, "Oh, I'm very interested!" Then say:

What do you think is holding you back? Is there some more information that I can give you?

What about just giving it a try?

****

One piece of advice about recruiting bears repetition. I previously mentioned "pockets of time." When used well, those pockets of time bring lots of success to your home-based business in recruiting and building your team.

If you are at home during the day, make one call each hour from 9:00 AM until 4:00 PM, and then one call at 7:00 PM and one at 8:00 PM. You will be making ten contacts a day, 50 contacts a week, 200 contacts a month. You will have many new representatives joining you and lots of selling events on your calendar. You will be well on your way to building a successful business!

Chapter 9

Creating a Work Environment

149

Chapter 9

Creating a Work Environment

One purpose of this book is to help you understand that **you are a professional.** Professionals have a place to work—a place they call their own in which they can conduct business. That place can be anything from a full-blown office to a separate room in your house to your favorite corner, just so long as it is conducive to your conducting business with the right business attitude.

When my kids were young and I was just starting my business, I worked in the middle of the family room, sitting on the floor at the coffee table with a spiral notebook. (See Spiral Notebook in Appendix B.) There was a phone in my hand and a list of people I needed to contact on the coffee table. When I picked up that list, I was in my work mode, and that setting became my office. I was ready to conduct business. Even then, I was available to my children; often times I was in the center of the action. To make this work, I made liberal use of the hold or mute buttons on the phone (Look on your phone—you probably have them too.) when I had to referee one of my kid's "that's mine" battles or those excited happy noises.

With that hold or mute button, I was able to keep the callers out of the family fun and maintain, in their minds, a strictly business atmosphere. That hold button can also be a real recruiting tool at times. When you see that you are getting distracted from your call, and you are about to hit that hold button; say, "Could you please hold on for a minute? I just need to be a referee for a second."  When you are ready to return to the call, share with the other person that you feel so lucky that you have your own business. You can work from home **alongside** your children, tend to their needs when necessary, and still earn income for the family. Then go back to the conversation you had to interrupt and be glad that you have it all. As your children get older, they will understand, "When Mommy is on a business call we have to be quieter."

Let me suggest that you also make liberal use of your answering machine. While tied up on a family project, your answering machine becomes your secretary. Just be sure to check your messages as **soon** as you can and get back to the callers as soon as possible. Remember that it is service that people are seeking, and your prompt return of the call is really good service. I recall once my mother asked me to call a new friend of hers who wanted to buy my products. The friend told my mother she

had had several bad experiences with other sales
reps who never called her back.

Okay, now let's get deeper into the business
mode. Let's talk about some tools you need by **all**
your phones. For some of you this may be pretty
basic but believe me, this is one of the topics that
frequently comes up at my seminars. First, you
need pads by each of your phones and yes, you need
something to write with as well. Pads are much
better than those little scraps of paper that we can't
find just five minutes after
we write on them.
Remember that this is your
business pad so don't mix
the business messages with
that note about the gallon of
milk that you need to buy.
Want to be even more
efficient? Have post cards as well as your recruiting
and hostess packets near the phone so that you can
address them as you are speaking to the potential
customer. That way there are no lost addresses and
no copying errors and you will also save time.
When you hang up the phone, your package or post
card is ready to mail. Of course, you still have to
keep tabs on the information you're sending out so
that you can properly follow up.

When you get to that point where you can
take over a small corner of the room as your
"office," then you can add some other useful tools.
In my early days, I used portable files since I knew
my office location in the house could change from
week to week. In my files, I kept catalogs, order
forms, the names of prospects, current company
information I wanted to share with prospects, and
other types of information that would get lost if they
just laid in a pile.

When you find yourself piling up one page
on top of another, that have
no relation to each other; you
just have a pile of paper, not
a filing system. Piles of
paper don't earn money; they
just take up your time as you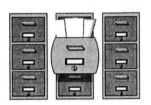
go through them when you're looking for
something. So, I would rather take the time to file
the paper once and always know where it is.

One more tip on how to avoid shuffling
paper unnecessarily. Try to work with each paper
only one time—when you pick it up, handle it right
then—it's not going to get better with age.
Moreover, reading it two or three times isn't going
to be helpful either. By dealing with it the first
time—that is, taking whatever action is necessary–

you will find the rewards come quicker. Think about your child's book bag and the last time you asked him or her to show you the parents' newsletter. *If* he or she found it, was it all in one piece? Watching the orderly way in which you set up your systems provides a wonderful example for your children.

By the way, when you find that the personal telephone line is being tied up by your business or that your business is being tied up by your personal calls, it's time to add a new telephone line. When you have that new business line, it should be considered *just that* and answered by someone old enough to make the callers feel that they have reached a business. You can picture your reaction if you called your favorite store and a four-year-old picked up the phone and said, "You don't sound like Grandma."

When you get that second phone line, you're on your way to needing a separate workspace that could be anywhere from using a spare room to converting your garage into a full-blown office as I did. You can see that as your business grows, your need for professional tools grows as well.

Don't be surprised if success brings you a computer. I couldn't live without mine. It's a given that you will need a fax machine and perhaps a copier and that one business telephone line could become two or three lines. Your printing expenses will increase as well as your postage expenses, but don't be intimidated by expenses. Wisely incurred expenses are an outgrowth of a successful business. When in doubt about whether spending additional money is worthwhile, ask yourself the question, "Will incurring this extra expense permit me to operate more efficiently and earn more money?" If the answer is yes, **go for it**.

Chapter 10

My Husband and My Father Speak Out

Chapter 10

My Husband and My Father Speak Out

A Husband's View

by Jim Meckley

I have found that most husbands are bottom-line kind of guys. What is important to them when you start a home-based business is:

- How is it going to affect me?

- How is it going to affect my family?

- Can you really make any money doing this?

159

Did you know that the answers to these questions all depend on you? I believe that husbands basically want to feel appreciated. If you tell them how much the business means to you and how much you appreciate their supporting you in your new business venture, you'll be off to a good start immediately.

My experience is that you can have a very successful home-based business without it negatively impacting your family. In fact, a home-based business can be the source of positive family growth. What better place is there to learn the importance of having a positive attitude, the importance of goal setting, and the importance of working a plan to reach a goal? What better place to learn the importance of marketing? Everyone needs marketing skills. How else does one get a date or a job?

The most important key to a successful home-based business as in a relationship is communication. Do you tell your husband why you love your business? Does he know your Purpose, Passion, and Plan for your business? If he does, then he will most likely be supportive of your business.

When Ilene started her home-based business, we had five children under twelve years old. Adena, our older daughter, was eleven; Stephanie was eight; David was six; Sammy was four; and Michael was just under two. I can honestly say that I never came home to a messy house. The kids were happy that Ilene was home after she had worked a full-time job for many years. Ilene was able to "keep up the house," take care of the kids, and work her business too! It was a matter of working her home-based business plan.

Husbands, us bottom-line kinds of guys, are interested to know how your business went, but beware of the "White Knight"! The "White Knight" is your husband who wants to rush in and solve your problems even when you may not really have a problem. If you come home at night after your presentation and complain about the number of guests who were there, the small amount of orders you received, or the hostess did not seem to appreciate what you did, you might hear the "White Knight" coming to the rescue with the suggestion, "So, why don't you just quit?"

Most husbands will try to solve their wife's "problems." Sometimes that *is* the problem. They will try to solve a problem even if you don't have a problem. You may just want to "vent" about what happened but he doesn't necessarily recognize that. He may see a problem and try to solve it. When that happens there are only two things you can do, hope he'll realize you are only venting or you can stop venting. I suggest that you keep a positive attitude and share the good things that are happening in your business not the negative.

Of course, it is easier to keep a positive attitude when you work your business. A home-based business only works when you work. Make a plan to accomplish some specific objectives during the day, then share your positive results with your husband. Set a goal that you would both like to accomplish so he can get excited with you about the progress you are making toward your goal. When Ilene first started her home-based business, I got excited about her earning an incentive trip to Hawaii. When your husband gets excited about a goal like I did, you will have a home-based business partner!

****

A Father's View

by Gerald Shur

 How your friends and relatives view your work in multi-level marketing is very much up to you. If you act professionally and take your work with a seriousness of purpose, then you will be regarded as a professional. As a lawyer for over 40 years and a manager of lawyers for much of that time, I can tell you that I have seen some lawyers who were not "professional" in their work habits. They were sloppy in the handling of their daily responsibilities, failed to set goals and expectations with respect to their assignments, and as a result, they generally achieved mediocre results. It was their work habits that did them in and no one would consider them professional. But, in Ilene, I have seen the consummate professional, an organized, goal-oriented person who sets and meets her expectations.

Oh, in the beginning of her career, no doubt just like many of you, she was inexperienced and had to go through the pains and anxieties of learning how to be a businesswoman while at the same time raising my five grandchildren. Let me assure you the children never suffered—they always came first; indeed, the entire family came first—husband, parents and the large extended family. Yet, with all that, she honed her skills, gained that necessary experience, overcame her anxieties, and became the true professional she is today. In the Random House Webster's College Dictionary, "professional" is defined as "following an occupation as a means of livelihood... **A salesman has to be a professional optimist."** That means, my friends, that just as Ilene is, you too are true professionals.

"Professional optimist"—think about it—that is a philosophy that Ilene has espoused throughout her career. She always has believed in setting goals, and she always has believed her goals are attainable. Indeed, we share the same philosophy that for every problem there must be a solution; perhaps we haven't found that solution yet, but we believe it is somewhere out there. Every successful person must believe in herself or himself, in the work she or he has chosen to do and in her or his ability to conquer those problems that will come her or his way. And that is what being a professional is all about.

To find those solutions to your business problems can often be challenging but, if you believe that a solution exists *somewhere* through hard work and inquiry (by, for example, using this book and Ilene's tapes and seminars), you can find that solution. Now there is nothing wrong with being a professional optimist. I sure would rather be a professional optimist than a professional pessimist. How many salespeople have you seen with negative attitudes that have been successful at anything? It's the positive people, like Ilene, who achieve true success and true happiness in their careers and in their lives.

There are no limits to Ilene's success just as there are none to yours. If you believe you **can**, you **will**. I know that to be true; I have watched Ilene grow from a novice saleswoman into one of the country's leading experts in multi-level marketing while, at the same time my grandchildren have all been very successful and very happy achievers in school. If you can forgive me for being the bragging grandfather, and speaking for the even more bragging grandmother, when you have a granddaughter working on her Doctorate in Psychology, another about to receive her Bachelor's in Social Work, a grandson in college  who was just elected to a national math honors society, a grandson who is about to begin college having been involved in more high school activities than I can remember, and finally our youngest grandson whose grades are outstanding and is well on his way to making a name for himself, you cannot help but brag. But, we don't forget that the attitude they display towards their work comes from the professionalism demonstrated by their mother and their father. I strongly believe that Ilene's ability to work out of her home has set a compelling example for her children of how "work" should be approached. As a result they have all achieved wonderful results. You, too, can have the same rewards—just take Ilene's lead.

Chapter 11

Finally,

It's Up

to You

Chapter 11

Finally, It's Up to You

Are you ready for a check up from the neck up?

Your Purpose, Passion, and Plan can make such a difference in your approach to your business. Without the three Ps, it can be easy to let other things get in the way of your business. However, when you are clear about your three Ps, there is nothing that will stop you from being a real success!

Are you communicating your goals to your family and friends?

How many people are you sharing with each day?

Are you inviting everyone to join you or take some action (such as buying or hostessing) and not just announcing?

Are you making people feel special by telling them that you would really love to have them on your team?

Are you asking lots of questions to help others become confident and feel good about making the choice to join you?

Are you proud of the way your spiral notebook looks?

Are you helping your new recruits develop a Purpose, Passion, and Plan for their business?

Are you prepared with a confident answer when someone asks you what you do?

What kind of pictures are you painting to share the enthusiasm you have for your business?

Are you determined, focused, and committed to being sure that you never prejudge, never make decisions for people, and always share the opportunity?

Are you making good use of your time? When used well, pockets of time bring lots of success in your home-based business.

My *purpose* in writing this book is not only to share my *passion* about network marketing with you but also to help you *plan* your career. As you have seen, these are the three Ps by which I have lived and become a successful salesperson. By following the techniques I have laid out, you too will enjoy the three Ps that will take you up, up and away. Remember it is now your job to *share and care* with others as I have done with you.

Appendix A

Action Plan

You have to know where you are going and how you are going to get there. An Action Plan is just your business map. Repeating an activity for 21 days makes it a habit. Commit to the Action Plan below for 21 days, and then it will be something you will incorporate into your life and business forever.

I will make _____ contacts per day.

I will get _____ referrals per day.

I will have _____ sales for the month.

I will hand out _____ business cards per week.

I will have _____ people in my recruiting pool at all times. (A recruiting pool is a list of people in the decision-making process of whether or not to give your business a try.)

I will have _____ recruits join me every month.

My daily prospecting plan is _____.

Appendix B

SPIRAL

NOTEBOOK

(Keeping track of the customers who come through your business every day)

How many customers come through your business each day? You can bring the customers to your business. You don't have to wait for them to come to you.

I developed this very simple system as a log to keep me accountable each day and to insure that I was touching my business every day.

At the top of each page of your notebook, put the dates for the next thirty days. This way if someone asks you to call them back or you need to schedule a follow-up call, you can turn to the page with that date and write a reminder to call them.

Number down the left-hand side (a minimum of from one to ten).

After each completed **full-service call** (You've invited them to be a new representative, hostess, or customer.), list the name of the person to whom you spoke with a brief summary of your conversation. For example, Mary Smith - interested in hosting, NI (not interested) in joining. Jane Doe – NI now, ck in spring.

At the end of the day, use a **highlighter** to mark all positive, future business responses. You will see on some days it may be the eighth, ninth or tenth response. You will see lots of results when looking back over each week from your minimum of **fifty** contacts.

Be sure to count the same person only once even if you speak to her more than once during the week. You are only hurting yourself if you do count her more than once. It is important that at least five contacts be new contacts that you've just met or people you've not talked to since the last news you had to share such as a new catalog, hostess promotion, or recruiting promotion.

Keep in mind a good full service call should take *no more than five minutes.* It will only be longer if you are working with the contact as a hostess, taking an order, or if she has expressed interest in becoming a member of your sales team.

You will feel **so** good each day when you see the page completed, and you will know that you did a good day's work. This method kept me on track balancing my family and my growing business.

Appendix C

Success
Quotes

"If you think you can or think you can't, you're right."

Henry Ford

"Whatever the mind can conceive and believe, the mind can achieve."

Napoleon Hill

"What you will do matters. All you need is to do it."

Judy Grahn

"We are what we repeatedly do. Excellence, then, is not an act, but a habit."

Aristotle

"Work hard at your chosen profession. People who seek your time and your services should feel rewarded for choosing you.

"The decision to trust yourself and your ability to support yourself is exactly that, a decision. If you refuse to be immobilized by fear and doubt and continue to do everything you know how to do to succeed, you will discover the ultimate security—knowledge that you can well make it on your own.

"Set up routines to take care of details automatically. Routines enable you to make a habit of taking care of minutiae in the quickest and least intrusive way. Once established, they enable you to take care of many details without even thinking about them."

The Secrets of Self-Employment

"You can get everything you want in life if you just help enough people get what they want."
Zig Ziglar

"To become, you have to overcome."
Anonymous

"To manage yourself, become familiar with yourself—your whims, your needs, your emotions, your patterns, your preferences, your strengths and weaknesses. Literally feed yourself the exact words, schedules, eating routines, and resources you need to nourish your competence and enable you to operate consistently at your best."

Making it On Your Own

"In the last analysis, what we are communicates far more eloquently than anything we say or do."

Stephen Covey,
The 7 Habits of Highly
Effective People

"Recruiting starts with *Sharing and Caring!*"

Ilene Meckley

Appendix D

Suggested Reading List

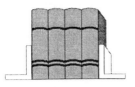

Anthony Robbins, a motivational speaker, talks about C.A.N.E.I.–Constant and Never-Ending Improvement. I feel that it is important to take time to read and listen to tapes as a part of your everyday routine. Listed below are a few of my favorites. Start your business library and make sure that you are continually adding to it.

Success is a Choice, Rick Pitino

Notes from a Friend, Anthony Robbins

Dare to Win, Jack Canfield & Mark Victor Hanson

The Winner Within, Pat Riley

Feel the Fear and Do It Anyway, Susan Jeffers, PhD

Making Your Dreams Come True, Marcia Wieder

The Aladdin Factor, Jack Canfield & Mark Victor Hanson

See You at the Top, Zig Ziglar

The 7 Habits of Highly Effective People, Stephen Covey

 Thanks for purchasing this book. Please call, write, or e-mail me if you would like to schedule a training seminar. Would you like to be on my free *Sharing and Caring* Link with recruiting tips and ideas? Just send your request to be added to the Link to the e-mail address below.

You may order additional copies of this book, my audiotapes, and our coloring/story book by calling 800-383-2039 or faxing/mailing an order to me.

Ilene Meckley
P. O. Box 1251, Bowie, MD 20715-1251
Telephone 301-262-2039 or 800-383-2039
E-mail: kidgifts@puff.dsport.com
Fax: 410-741-1093

Recruiting Starts With *Sharing and Caring*
$12.00 per audiotape, 2 or more $10 per tape

Getting Down To Business In Your Home-Based Business
$12.00 per audiotape, 2 or more $10 per tape

Just Like Mom coloring/story book
$3.00 per book, minimum order five

Sharing and Caring—**The Key to Taking Your Business Up, Up, and Away!**
$15 per copy, 5 or more $12 per copy

Shipping and handling 10% of order

Please add State Sales Tax (in Maryland only)

Make checks payable to **Ilene Meckley**.

We accept VISA, MasterCard, Discover, and American Express.